TOWARDS A NEW IRELAND

TOWARDS
A NEW IRELAND

Garret FitzGerald, T.D., Ph.D.
Barrister at Law

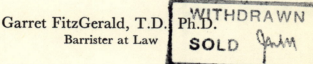

CHARLES KNIGHT & CO. LTD.
LONDON
1972

Charles Knight & Co. Ltd.
11/12 Bury Street, London EC3A 5AP
Dowgate Works, Douglas Road, Tonbridge

Reprinted 1972

ISBN 0 85314 161 4

Reprinted in Great Britain by
Lewis Reprints Ltd.
Member of Brown Knight & Truscott Group
London and Tonbridge

Contents

To the
'New Irelanders',
North and South,
Protestant and Catholic

Preface

THIS book was started in August, 1971, but the great bulk of it was written in the early months of 1972. Inevitably in a situation evolving so rapidly, and so unpredictably, some of it may be dated by the time it is published. This is not, however, an attempt to unravel the events of Northern Ireland since 1968; indeed only passing reference is made to these events. Instead the book endeavours to trace the causes of the political division of Ireland; to examine how this political division proved in some measure self-perpetuating, as each of the two parts of Ireland developed in its separate way; and to consider how this political division might eventually be resolved in such a way that both communities living in the island of Ireland would find themselves united in common allegiance to a society which both would find acceptable. The book is written from the standpoint of a citizen of the Republic, who desires the political reunification of Ireland. But it seeks to avoid chauvinism, and tries to see the problem from the dual standpoints of the Northern Protestant tradition and the Irish nationalist tradition.

I owe a debt of gratitude to three Northerners who at short notice read the first draft and helped me to eliminate from it some of its defects—Canon Eric Elliott, John Simpson, and Terry Stewart. No one should blame them for any errors or false emphases or wrong conclusions that remain; all such are the author's fault alone.

On terminology several points must be made. First of all for the sake of brevity I have referred to the Roman Catholic Church and its members as 'Catholic' *tout court*; I trust my Protestant friends who also share the sense of being part of the universal church which the word 'Catholic' implies, will accept that this abbreviation involves no reflection on them or their Church.

vii

Secondly, I have used the word 'pluralist' or 'pluralism' at several points. This is not intended to refer to a caste-type society, in which different religious groups would be subject to different civil laws. It is used to describe a society within which people of different religious, cultural or linguistic traditions would be treated as equal citizens, and subjected to no disability because they did not share the tradition of a majority of the population.

1. Why Partition?

THE BACKGROUND

The historical origins of the Northern Ireland problem are by now familiar to anyone interested in the subject. It would be tedious to recount this historical background in detail yet again. In this first chapter, therefore, of a book dedicated to analysing the Northern Ireland situation with a view to seeing how it can best be solved peacefully within an all-Ireland context, only a few key points will be mentioned before going on to examine some of the underlying causes of the political division of Ireland.

The North-East corner of Ireland and nearby Scotland have been closely linked since man came to live in these regions of north-western Europe, remote from the areas where the human species originated and first flourished.

In historical times the links have been close—much of Scotland having been colonised from Ireland over a thousand years ago, while the coastal areas of Ulster nearest to Scotland were re-colonised by Scottish families before the Ulster plantation in the early 1600s—which, incidentally, affected the areas of Ulster away from the north-east coast.

This plantation, unlike its predecessors further south, proved long-lasting. The new inhabitants, Lowland Scots and English, obtained and retained the best land of the province, although their tenure did not become secure until after the Williamite War towards the end of the century. The seventeenth century struggle between colonists and natives was marked by atrocities on both sides, the memory of which proved enduring—and by deeds of heroism, such as the Protestant defence of Derry, which provided the settlers with myths and legends to bolster their morale in centuries to come.

In the eighteenth century the Presbyterian colonists suffered

1

with the Catholics they had displaced, at the hands of the Anglican regime of penal laws. At the end of the century the two oppressed religions briefly made common cause, in the Rebellion of 1798, but the campaign for Catholic Emancipation, threatening with more numerous Catholic votes the whole Protestant position in Ireland, led to a new alliance between Presbyterians and Anglicans, which was to last. As the nineteenth century progressed, communal violence between Catholics and Protestants became common, leading to the suppression of the Orange Order and its demonstrations for a period.

The Fenian Movement and the extension of the franchise in 1872 may have heightened the fears of Protestants, especially as it was followed by the emergence for the first time of an effective Home Rule Party, which in the 1880s under Parnell dominated Irish politics, and disrupted the British parliamentary scene. The alliance between the British Conservative Party and the Northern Orangemen was forged in that decade, when Lord Randolph Churchill decided to 'play the Orange card'. Less than thirty years later this alliance brought Britain itself close to civil war, as the leaders of the Conservative Party plotted with the Ulster Unionists to resist Home Rule, and involved the British Army itself in their schemes. The consequent 'Curragh Mutiny' was followed by a weakening of the Liberal Party's determination to give Home Rule to the whole of Ireland, and the seeds of Partition were sown in the years from 1912 to 1914, when a provision for a temporary 'opting out' by part of the province of Ulster came under discussion as a compromise between apparently irreconcilable positions.

The Great War brought this violent debate to a sudden end, and when it was resumed towards the end of the War, the shadow of the 1916 Rebellion loomed over the discussions. Irish aspirations were heightened by delay, a lesson from which British Governments might have learnt—but did not learn—something to help them with their handling of the Northern Ireland problem from 1968 onwards. Dominion status for twenty-six of thirty-two counties failed to satisfy a big minority of Irishmen in 1922, provoking a bitter civil war within the territory of what later became the Republic. And whatever hopes there might have been of persuading Ulster Protestants to accept participation in a united Home Rule Ireland, fully represented in the UK Parliament, there was little hope of securing a peaceful transition to a united Irish Dominion in 1922.

Thereafter little changed. If Kevin O'Higgins, the Deputy-Premier of the Irish Free State who was assassinated in 1927, had lived he might, perhaps, have made headway with his proposal—discussed secretly with the Ulster leader, Lord Carson—for a Dual Monarchy, uniting North and South within a separate Irish Kingdom, although the force of the republican legend, sanctified by 1916, would have made this solution difficult of acceptance in the South. With O'Higgins's death even this hope evaporated, however, and the advent to power of Mr. De Valera's Fianna Fail Government in 1932, nine short years after they had been defeated in the Civil War, made the prospect of reunification on agreed terms even more remote. The new Constitution adopted by the South in 1937, containing elements of visibly Catholic inspiration, and omitting any reference to the Crown, drove a further wedge between the two parts of Ireland, and Irish neutrality in the Second World War finally consolidated the political division. Thereafter, until the rise of the Civil Rights Movement in Northern Ireland in 1968, a stalemate prevailed.

Some at least of the reasons why only part of Ireland became independent in 1922, thus creating the problem of Partition, are implicit in the historical account above. But before going on to examine the effects that this division of the island has had on its subsequent development, economic, social, political and cultural, the origins of Partition need to be probed more deeply. Several aspects in particular deserve further consideration and analysis.

ECONOMIC FACTORS

Inadequate attention is often given to the economic basis of Partition. It would be wrong to suggest that economic divergences between the north-east of Ireland and the remainder made a political division inevitable; but without subscribing to undiluted economic determinism, it is nevertheless possible to attribute considerable importance to economic factors in accounting for the political division of the country after 1920.

The different evolution of industry in the north-east corner of Ireland and in the rest of the country had its origins in the seventeenth century, when the linen industry became well established in the north-east. In the past this development has sometimes been explained as having been due to a combination of alleged Government discrimination in favour of the more

Protestant part of the country, and a different type of land-holding in Ulster. (This form of tenure gave greater security to tenants and therefore encouraged better husbandry, this in turn facilitating capital formation, and fostering qualities of diligence which proved valuable when transferred from agriculture to industry.) This theory about the origins of industrial development in the north-east has been described by one authority as 'largely irrelevant', and that part of it that involves deliberate discrimination in favour of the Protestant north-east is difficult to sustain in the light of the efforts made to foster the industry outside Ulster by the Board of Trustees for the Linen and Hempen Manufacturers, established by the exclusively Protestant Irish Parliament in 1711. The same authority—Mr. W. H. Crawford[1]—remarks that 'without the active encouragement of the Board, however, serious efforts would not have been made to establish the industry outside the province of Ulster'.

Mr. Crawford goes on to attribute the concentration of the linen industry in the north-east to the fact that much of the area was re-settled after the Cromwellian wars by skilled workers from England, whose industrial background encouraged them to engage in linen production during slack periods on their farms and of whom only the most enterprising survived in the poor and disturbed economy of Ulster at that period. These immigrants were supplemented by Huguenot textile workers from Flanders and France—refugees from religious persecution —who were later settled in several areas. Partly because of its earlier start in this region, and partly because of the way in which it was organised—spinning and weaving (operations involving little capital), being carried out by small holders who could survive the ups and downs of the industry—the linen industry prospered in Ulster. In many parts of the south, on the other hand, its spread was artificially fostered at a later stage on a vertically integrated basis that was more vulnerable to fluctuations in trade. The depression of 1773 thus hit the industry in Leinster and Connaught much more severely than in Ulster.

The Industrial Revolution undermined the prosperity of most other Irish industries, owing to the absence of coal deposits in Ireland equivalent to those which provided the foundation of British prosperity in this period, and especially in the first

---

[1] 'The Rise of the Linen Industry', by W. H. Crawford. The second of a series of Thomas Davis Lectures, published in *The Formation of the Irish Economy*, Mercier Press, Cork, 1969.

decades of the nineteenth century.[2] The removal of protection in 1824 and the deflation caused by the amalgamation of the Irish and British currencies in 1826 aggravated the situation brought about by the Industrial Revolution in Britain and the development of cheaper steamship services between Britain and Ireland, which facilitated an expansion of imports from Britain. The linen industry was almost alone in surviving in this situation, at the cost of a drastic rationalisation which replaced the traditional structure of the industry based on smallholding spinners by powered flax-spinning, concentrated largely in Belfast, although weaving continued to be carried out throughout the countryside for several further decades—power-loom weaving not making its appearance until after the Famine.

The concentration of Irish industrialisation in Belfast was taken a stage further in the middle of the nineteenth century with the development of shipbuilding in that city. Intelligent planning by Belfast Harbour Commissioners who provided facilities for ship-building and repairing, pressure on space on Mersey-side as the expansion of the Liverpool docks crowded out shipbuilders in that area, and the fortuitous availability of a surplus of iron plates in Belfast as a result of an unsuccessful ironworks venture, provided the conditions for the emergence of a successful shipbuilding venture there during the 1850s.

The basic industries of linen and shipbuilding in the north-east were supplemented during the nineteenth century by a variety of other engineering industries and by the development of clothing trades. As a result, by the time the Home Rule Bill was introduced into the Westminster Parliament, the north-east corner of Ireland had become an industrialised area, whose prosperity depended largely on free trade for its linen manufactures and on a close link with Britain for its shipbuilding industry. By contrast the rest of Ireland had little industry of consequence apart from a not very prosperous food-processing sector, and the best prospect for industrial development outside the north-east appeared to lie in a period of industrial protection. Protection it was felt would provide the conditions in which new industries could be established, and, hopefully, these industries would within a generation or so reach a stage of maturity that would enable them to survive in competitive conditions.

By the early years of this century, therefore, the North-East

[2] 'The Industrialisation of the North-East', by J. M. Goldstrom in *The Formation of the Irish Economy*, Mercier Press, Cork, 1969.

and the rest of Ireland had markedly divergent economic interests, which pulled them politically in different directions. Even if this polarisation had not been accompanied by a politico-religious division between the Protestant minority concentrated in the north-east and the Catholic majority in the rest of Ireland there would, therefore, have been an economic basis for a temporary political division of Ireland that would enable the bulk of the country to achieve a measure of industrialisation behind protective tariffs, while leaving the north-east in a continuing, close free trade relationship with Great Britain.

How important a part did these economic considerations play in the events that led up to the division of Ireland in the Government of Ireland Act, 1920, which for the first time gave legislative expression to a concept that had emerged as a real issue in the Home Rule controversy immediately before the Great War? On the surface the impetus towards a Partition solution would seem to have been political and religious rather than economic, but economic forces have a habit of working under the surface of events, providing a ground-swell that is often un-noticed by those who are preoccupied with the froth on the waves. Was this the case in this instance? Perhaps not. Perhaps the forces of blind religious prejudice and the desire of two religiously distinct communities in the north-east of Ireland in the one case to maintain and in the other to destroy a relationship of privilege and dominance that existed between them, were in reality as well as in appearance the most powerful forces at work in the minds of the mass of the people in this area. But it is not certain that these forces would in fact have achieved a political division of a hitherto politically-united country had it not been for the coincidence of regional economic interests with the religious and political forces at work.

In Northern Ireland the support of the respectable Protestant business community for the by no means entirely constitutional anti-Home Rule movement might not have been so easily forthcoming had it not been for a clear conviction on their part that their pockets as well as their prejudices would be best served by opting out of Home Rule. And the financial and moral support of this business community both heightened the morale of the popular movement aganist Home Rule in this area and provided it with the necessary financial backing, as well as impressing the British authorities that in the anti-Home Rule lobby they were not dealing with men of straw.

In the rest of the country the economic opportunities that fiscal independence could provide were high-lighted in the propaganda of Sinn Fein and its supporters, but as these opportunities were to be reaped not by existing business interests (many of which, indeed, felt that their continued financial success depended on maintaining the free trade position with the UK) but by hypothetical industrialists of the future, this was a pamphleteering argument for the masses rather than an argument that brought any solid business or financial backing to the independence movement. Even at the level of propaganda it is possible that the economic argument that Ireland was over-taxed in the Union with Britain carried greater weight than the claim that Ireland's future prosperity depended upon securing the ability to protect infant industries. The divergent economic interests of the north-east vis-à-vis those of the rest of Ireland thus played an important but perhaps not a determining role in the division of Ireland in 1920, although in the absence of strong politico-religious forces working for such a division, the regional economic differences would have been most unlikely to have led to any such division.

The Religious Division

The origins of these politico-religious differences have been outlined earlier. The crucial element was the fact that the large-scale Ulster Plantation occurred *after* the Reformation, and that these colonists, unlike their predecessors in other parts of Ireland, were inhibited from cultural assimilation by their religious differentiation from the native population they partially displaced. This barrier to inter-marriage and the extreme ferocity of the partly religious wars of the seventeenth century in Ireland together ensured that by the outset of the eighteenth century there existed in much of the northern part of the island two clearly-differentiated peasant communities, co-existing in enmity, with bitter memories to be cherished in folk tradition. Elsewhere in Ireland outside the capital, Dublin, which had a large Protestant as well as Catholic working-class population, the religious differences were largely class differences; the land-owning class were Protestant, and the peasants were Catholic. But while this did nothing to ensure inter-class harmony, it at least avoided the kind of situation that existed in much of the north of the Island, where the classic ingredients for communal strife existed within the peasant class itself. There the Protestant peasants, conscious of the fact that the title to their land was by right of conquest, and that it was not accepted by the former owners, and keeping alive from one generation to the next their recollection of violent attempts by the Catholics to displace them during the seventeenth century, feared and consequently hated their Catholic neighbours—whom they also regarded with the contempt of conquerors for conquered. The Catholics on the other hand had not been completely displaced by the Plantation: many of them had remained in Ulster, scratching out a living on the poorer land, and nursing a grudge against those who had deprived them of the acres they had held from time immemorial.

In this situation and given the total barrier to assimilation of the two communities posed by the religious differences, it is not surprising, perhaps, that even three-and-a-half centuries later the communal bitterness persists. It is true that at one period it had seemed as if the simple polarisation of Protestant versus Catholic might have broken down, because of the deep split within the Protestant community between Anglicans and Presbyterians, and the exclusion by the dominant Anglicans of Presbyterians as well as Catholics from the full rights of citizenship. A common resentment against Anglican dominance brought Catholics and Presbyterians together in the closing decades of the eighteenth century, culminating in the explosion of 1798 where in different parts of Ireland both of these religious groups broke into rebellion under leaders largely inspired by the French Revolution. But this alliance did not survive to the middle of the nineteenth century. It found some echoes, it is true, in the mixed Protestant and Catholic leadership of the 1848 rebellion, but by the time that Rebellion took place, the mass of Presbyterians had become firmly aligned with the Anglicans against the Catholic minority; Catholic emancipation was a watershed in Irish history, producing a permanent polarisation of forces along Protestant-Catholic lines which its promoters perhaps never foresaw. Thereafter while there were always individual Protestants, and especially Presbyterians, who found themselves in sympathy with the nationalist aspirations of the Catholic majority, the great bulk of Presbyterians as well as Anglicans, linked together, in the north especially, by the Orange Order and its associated movements (e.g. the Apprentice Boys and the Royal Black Preceptory), were firmly aligned in favour of the maintenance of the Union with Britain.

Moreover a new element was introduced into the situation with the rapid growth of the Catholic population of Belfast in the first half of the nineteenth century, which, especially after 1850, gave rise to religious riots in the city and to a process of self-segregation in Catholic and Protestant working-class quarters.[3]

THE IMPACT OF 1916

If Catholic emancipation was a turning-point in Irish history, so of course, was 1916. We cannot know how events might have turned out if this Rebellion had not taken place. It is difficult, however, in the light of the history of the British Empire since the Great War to resist the thesis that if Ireland had remained peaceful throughout the Great War, Home Rule must have been conceded after the War in terms which would inevitably have involved an evolution towards complete independence, and it has been argued that the conditions with respect to Northern Ireland in any such Home Rule settlement could not have been more prejudicial to political unity than those contained in the Anglo-Irish settlement of 1921, subsequently part-confirmed and part-varied by the Boundary Commission Agreement of four years later. Thus Dr. Conor Cruise O'Brien has commented 'I believe that the political independence *of a 26-county State*—which is what we have—could and would have been obtained peacefully on the basis of the Home Rule proposals reluctantly accepted by the Irish Party in 1914. The subsequent armed struggle was waged not to bring our present 26-county State into being but to *avert* substantially that outcome, adumbrated in the proposals of 1914. This recourse to violence was a failure. It ended in the acceptance by a majority of the Dail and of the people of a settlement based in substance though not in form on Lloyd George's 'Parliament of Southern Ireland' which in turn was essentially what was offered to Redmond in 1914. Subsequent improvements on the Treaty settlement were won by negotiation and could, obviously, have been won in the same way on the basis of the 1914 Home Rule proposals'.[4]

Many would go beyond this to argue that if 1916 had not happened it might have been possible to have secured a post-war settlement whose provisions in respect of Northern Ireland would have been designed to ensure that any autonomy ac-

[3] *A Social Geography of Belfast*, by Emrys Jones, OUP 1960, pp. 189 *et seq.*
[4] Letter to *Irish Times*, July 24, 1971.

corded to that area would not have involved the possibility of a permanent political division of the island, but this must be speculative.

In view of the apparently unending chain of violence unleashed in 1916, this assessment, which might be described as the 'Redmondite' view of recent Irish history, will have an attraction for many people. In fairness the case for 1916 must also be put.

Those who launched this Rebellion were not thinking in terms of different degrees of independence, to be achieved by alternative dates, with varying options for a temporarily separate Northern Ireland. Their vision was a different and more fundamental one, their preoccupations much more long-term. The mood of those who refused to follow Redmond at the outbreak of the Great War in 1914 was many years later described by the author's father in these terms: 'I think that our first reaction (to the outbreak of the Great War) was one of jubilation. England would now be beaten and a resurgent Irish nationalism would assert and make effective our claim to real autonomy. Whatever degree of exultation possessed us soon gave way to a condition very close to despair. On the very declaration of War, Mr. Redmond made a statement assuring the English people that the Irish Volunteers would protect Ireland. But more disturbing than that mere statement was the fact that it immediately became apparent that it really represented the views of the majority of the Irish people.

'The movement on which all our dreams had centred seemed merely to have canalised the martial spirit of the Irish people for the defence of England. Our dream castles toppled about us with a crash. It was brought home to us that the very fever that had possessed us was due to a subconscious awareness that the final end of the Irish nation was at hand. For centuries England had held Ireland materially. But now it seemed that she held her in a new and utterly complete way. Our national identity was obliterated not only politically, but also in our own minds. The Irish people had recognised themselves as part of England.'[5]

To those who reacted in this way to the events in Ireland that accompanied the outbreak of the Great War, an armed uprising appeared as the last and only hope of reviving the flickering flame of an apparently almost extinguished national spirit.

[5] *The Autobiography of Desmond FitzGerald*, Routledge and Kegan Paul, 1969.

Even if they had had the foresight to assess accurately the way in which Ireland had since evolved, and even if they had believed that their actions would contribute to a political division of the Irish nation for a period of not less than half a century, perhaps much longer—can we be sure that this would have deterred them from a course of action which they saw as justified in terms of several millennia of Irish history? Might they not have maintained their determination, preferring to pursue what they saw as a last chance of keeping the spirit of Irish Nationalism alive, rather than to follow a course which, while it might have been more conductive to the preservation of Irish unity and peace during the twentieth century, might in their judgment have left Ireland united to Britain in aspirations and cultural outlook as well as united politically within its own boundaries?[6]

This is the central issue of modern Irish history, and it is one on which historians are likely to remain divided. The state of Irish nationalism in 1914, and the extent to which a blood sacrifice was necessary to re-kindle its spirit, are matters so intangible as to defy a conclusive historical judgment. We can never know whether a Home Rule Ireland would on the one hand have been so lacking in any sense of nationality as to have evolved into a pale carbon copy of the neighbouring island, as the men of 1916 feared, or whether the authors of 1916 exaggerated this risk in their own minds and, had they held their hand, would have seen the emergence in the post-war period of a Home Rule Ireland which even if divided would have been subject only to a limited and temporary division, and been fully capable of evolving peacefully into a united sovereign State. All we can do is recognise that to different groups of people at that time each of these theses seemed valid, and provided them with what they felt to be legitimate bases for action.

What concerns us today, however, is the effect that 1916 and its immediate consequences have had on the relations between the two parts of Ireland. For most Irish people 1916 became in the years that followed the basis of a new concept of nationalism. It can, of course, be argued that this Rebellion was only the last of a long series of attempts to establish Irish independence by physical force, and that it therefore involved nothing new. But because of its peculiarly dramatic character, the subsequent

[6] For a fuller treatment of this see 'The Significance of 1916', by Garret FitzGerald, *Studies*, Spring, 1966.

execution of its leaders, and the way in which it led within five years to the establishment of an independent—albeit truncated —Irish State, 1916 came to have a significance for most Irish people that transcends that of all previous revolts against British rule. This last rebellion had been intended to create a new myth, and so in fact it did. But this myth, which within a few years united the physical force and constitutional traditions in Irish nationalism, simultaneously had the effect of creating an even deeper division than that which had formerly existed between the nationalist and unionist traditions. The new nationalism created by 1916 owed much of its strength—perhaps even its existence—to the language movement of the late nineteenth and early twentieth centuries. In seeking to repay this debt, and, indeed, in seeking to give concrete shape to the aspirations of the men of 1916 who had been trying to re-kindle what they felt to be a dying Irish nationalism, those who inherited the mantle of the executed leaders did in fact create a new Ireland much more alien to the Northern Protestants than the kind of Ireland that had existed before the Great War.

The full implications of this were never perhaps considered. The men who planned the Rising had been too concerned to prevent the flame of nationalism from being extinguished to consider in any detail whether this flame could ever blaze up in a manner that would make it acceptable to the Ulstermen who light a thousand bonfires on the night of each 11th of July. If the 1916 leaders thought at all about this problem, they may have allowed themselves to be deceived into placing an altogether distorted emphasis on the occasional Ulster Protestant who even in the early twentieth century showed some interest in Gaelic culture or traditions or in Irish nationalism, or they may have given much more weight to the non-sectarian nationalism of 1798 than could be carried by that tradition which had been over-shadowed by the Catholic Emancipation movement before it could strike deep roots. But, whatever they may or may not have thought on this subject, the fact is that the men of 1916 created a new myth, or re-furbished an old one, in terms that have subsequently proved divisive between North and South. 1916 to-day stands as a psychological barrier between Protestant Ulster and the predominantly Catholic rest of Ireland. What to a majority of the Irish people has become sacred, is to the Northern Protestant to-day an alien and even hateful tradition.

GUERILLA WARFARE AND POGROM IN THE NORTH 1920–1922

The effects of the establishment of an incomplete 1916-orientated Irish State upon attitudes North and South of the Border in the years following 1920 will be further considered in the next chapter. Here we are concerned only with the reasons why Ireland was divided in 1920 in a manner that has proved disturbingly long-lived. To this division the violence of the Anglo-Irish struggle from 1919 to 1921, which was carried on in Northern Ireland as actively as in the rest of the country, was another important contributory factor.

Most historical attention in the Republic has been focused upon the guerilla warfare in the South—even the War of Independence has in a sense been partitioned! In Northern Ireland this War had an extra dimension, however, for in much of the North, and especially in Belfast, it had to be carried on in predominantly hostile territory. At the very time when in the South many Unionists were becoming alienated from British rule by the indiscriminate violence of the Black and Tans, and when Volunteers on the run sometimes found shelter in safe Unionist houses, the Northern campaign was degenerating into sectarian warfare as the working-class Protestant population in Belfast joined with gusto in the Black-and-Tan campaign against the Volunteers.

When the Truce came in mid-1921 the Belfast pogrom against Catholics blamed for the violent actions of the IRA was in full swing. At no period was violence more brutal, senseless or universal in Belfast than at that time, and whatever possibility there might have been of securing a peaceful transition to Home Rule for the whole of Ireland seven years earlier, there was none whatever by the time the Treaty came to be signed. The rift between Catholics and Protestants in the north-east had by then been filled with too much blood for any form of Irish unity to be possible at that time without provoking inter-community massacres.

THE BELIEF THAT PARTITION MUST BE TEMPORARY

One other factor contributing to the acceptance of Partition in the Treaty of 1921 must also be mentioned. No one believed that Partition could be other than very temporary. To a people who have now experienced this political division for over half-a-century, such a belief may appear irrational. We in this generation see this situation in the light of hindsight, however.

To those who faced the problem in 1921, the idea of a long-lasting partition of a country which had never previously experienced this kind of division seemed ludicrous. *They* had always known Ireland as one country, with one administration centred in Dublin although, of course, subordinated to the British Parliament. Every vocational and religious body was then organised on an all-Ireland basis. No one had ever thought seriously of organising Irish affairs on any other basis. In these conditions on arrangement under which the north-east could opt out of the new Irish State was not conceived by most people as anything other than a temporary expedient to ensure the establishment of an independent Irish State without delay, and to minimise further bloodshed in Belfast pending a final settlement. There is reason to believe that it was not in the South alone that Partition was seen thus. Many Northern Protestants, whatever they may have said in public, shared the conviction that Ireland was by nature a single country. They saw Partition as a breathing-space rather than as a final solution—and many of them continued to feel this at least up to the Second World War. Even to-day, the deep-rooted but rarely admitted belief that ultimately Irish unity must prevail, lies at the heart of many Northern Protestant attitudes.

In the rest of the country this belief that Irish unity could not be sundered, but only temporarily delayed, underlay the Treaty Debate, whose most curious feature to Irishmen of a later generation was the virtual absence of any discussion of Partition, save on the part of Northern deputies like Sean MacEntee, and by contrast the almost neurotic concentration on that irrelevant anachronism, the Oath of Allegiance, which was disposed of without much fuss barely a decade later. Paradoxically Partition became a long-term feature of Irish life *because* most Irishmen believed it could never become so and consequently treated it less seriously than it deserved. Had even a significant minority taken it seriously, as something which if once allowed to happen would be very difficult to dislodge, events might have turned out very differently.

Many forces have thus contributed to the Partition of Ireland. The post-Reformation timing of the Ulster Plantation; the viciousness of the seventeenth century wars in Ulster; the almost chance development of a different pattern of economic activity in the North-East, leading to divergent economic interests between that area and the rest of the country; the 1916 Rising and the special character of the War of Independence in the North and especially in Belfast; and finally the inability of all concerned in 1920–1922 to conceive that there could be a prolonged division of the country—all these played their part and have combined to create an extraordinarily intractable political problem whose existence has, moreover, proved self-perpetuating.

2. Effects in the Republic

WHERE economic or cultural or ideological differences within a country lead to a political division on geographical lines the subsequent separate development of the two regions tends to aggravate these differences. The removal of the constraints on cultural or social diversity formerly provided by a single governmental and administrative system can in time have profound effects, powerfully reinforcing the initial act of partition. This is clearly true where the division involves ideological differences, as in Germany, Vietnam or Korea, but the Irish experience has shown that the same self-reinforcing divisive effects can operate where the initial partitioning derived from more long-established cultural or religious differences rather than ones of contemporary ideology.

Because the partitioning of Ireland arose from the failure of a nationalist movement to achieve independence for the whole of the national territory as defined by geography and history, the widening of the gap between the two parts of Ireland since 1920 has in large measure been due to the momentum of cultural change in the independent part of Ireland, where the successful nationalist movement sought to re-shape the destinies of that part of the country under its control. Other factors have also been at work, however. Because the division of the country segregated a predominantly Protestant North-East from an overwhelmingly Roman Catholic remainder, and because in Ireland religion has remained a vital cultural force retaining the loyalties of the masses in a manner that has not been true in much of the rest of Europe, the two parts of Ireland have evolved in different directions in matters such as education and legislation concerning public morality. Finally the nature of the financial arrangements between the Northern Ireland and

16

British Governments within the United Kingdom has been such that the development in the post-war period of British social welfare and agricultural policies, and of policies for regional industrial development, has involved a massive continuing transfer of resources from Great Britain to Northern Ireland, no parallel to which exists in the case of the Republic; this has widened a pre-existing gap between standards of living in the two parts of Ireland.

It must be said, however, that in certain other more limited ways Partition has had the effect of keeping the two areas moving along rather similar lines. Thus the failure of Irish politics to develop on ideological lines on either side of the Border owes something to the pervasive effects of the Partition issue. In the North the alignment of political forces for or against a united Ireland has certainly stunted the growth of ideological politics, while in the Republic the Partition issue has at least contributed to a similar situation.

Again a desire to avoid the creation of undue divergence between North and South has perceptibly influenced certain policies in the Republic, where sensitive cultural areas such as the Irish language and the teaching of history are not involved. Thus there has been an almost pathetic desire by governments in the Republic to avoid any differentiation between the North and the Republic—and, consequently, between Great Britain and the Republic—in such matters as currency and standard time. Similarly the Irish trade union movement has accepted a scale of activity by British unions in the Republic as well as in Northern Ireland which would scarcely have been tolerated but for the powerful incentive of retaining a united trade union movement for the whole island.

Finally, although this is less easy to demonstrate, there is reason to believe that the foreign policy of the Republic has been perceptibly influenced throughout much of its history as an independent state by a desire to maintain a relationship with the United Kingdom which would facilitate the eventual ending of Partition, even though at times this has laid the government of the day open to the accusation of slavishly following British policies, or at least failing to oppose such policies.

DIVISIVE EFFECTS OF CULTURAL CHANGE IN THE REPUBLIC

The national movement of the years from 1913 onwards was in large measure inspired by the language revival initiated in the closing years of the nineteenth century. This revival had been cultural rather than political in its origins; many of those who launched it were apolitical or even Unionist in politics, and few of its early sponsors saw in this cultural movement a method of arousing national feeling for political objectives. Yet together with the Anglo-Irish literary revival, associated with W. B. Yeats and the Abbey Theatre, the language revival had a profound political impact; coming after a long period of cultural vacuum, it instilled in many young people in the early years of this century a conviction that despite the anglicisation of the island in the nineteenth century, Ireland was the possessor of an ancient culture which must be preserved and revived for the benefit of future generations—a task that could successfully be undertaken only by an independent Irish State. To a generation whose parents had grown up in a country demoralised by the Famine, this cultural revival had a special importance, offering an inspiration where none had seemed to exist before.

The participants in the national movement, with few exceptions, were conscious of the debt they owed to this cultural movement, and especially to the Irish language revival. Their ability to repay this debt whole-heartedly was greatly weakened by the Civil War and the bitterness and cynicism which is left behind. By 1924 instead of a virile and self-confident community, setting unitedly about the task of creating a new State founded on an ancient culture, the independent part of Ireland was physically and morally crippled. But although the enthusiasm needed for a successful revival of Gaelic culture had evaporated in the ruined streets of Dublin and ambush-ridden hedgerows of rural Ireland between the summer of 1922 and the spring of 1923, the new Government nevertheless tackled energetically, if not always wisely, the task of repaying the nation's debt to the language revival movement of thirty years earlier. The new State was to be bilingual and the Irish language was to be revived through the schools. In 1924 it was decided that the Irish language should be an essential subject for the Intermediate Certificate examination by 1928. Ten years later another Government somewhat superfluously extended this requirement to the School Leaving Certificate, although by that time all but 5% of children completing their secondary school studies were already taking Irish as an examination subject. Irish was also made an essential subject for entry into and promotion within the administrative public service and tests in

Irish were also applied to candidates for professional posts in the public service. (Since 1910 Irish had been an essential subject for matriculation in the National University of Ireland—but this has never applied to Dublin University.)

These decisions were comprehensible against the background of the previous thirty years and in the context of a truncated 26-county State. But they undoubtedly raised a fresh barrier between the North and the rest of the country. The Irish language played no part in the traditions of the Northern majority, and while individual Northern Protestants had in the nineteenth century shown an interest in the Irish language and other aspects of Gaelic culture, these were exceptional cases. For almost the entire Northern Protestant population the steps taken to revive Irish in the Republic in the half-century since an Independent Irish State was founded have confirmed their prejudices against this State—especially as by making the Irish language an essential subject for school certificate examinations and for entrance to the public service, the Protestant population North and South, who had never shared the Gaelic tradition and whose ancestors had never been Irish-speaking, were in effect discriminated against and reduced, in their own eyes at least, to the rank of second-class citizens, excluded from full participation in the life of the independent Irish State, unless they adopted a tradition which was to them alien.

The existence of different and indeed mutually alien traditions within the island of Ireland would have posed a problem for a unified independent Irish State, had one come into existence. But within a State with over a million Protestants, as well as many Catholics especially in urban areas, who did not feel they shared in the Gaelic tradition, this difficulty would in practice have had to be resolved by a pluralist solution, recognising the validity of the different traditions—Ulster Scots, Anglo-Irish, and non-Gaelic urban—as well as the rural Gaelic tradition which was either Irish-speaking or at least removed by only a generation or two from the use of the language. It would have been inconceivable that within a united Ireland the Irish language could have been made essential for school certificates or for employment in the public service, against the interests and wishes of so many minorities, who indeed, might well have added up to a majority of the whole population.

Within a truncated Irish State, which excluded a million Protestants and the major industrial centre of Belfast, these

measures were, however, introduced without effective opposition or even serious questioning. The idea of a pluralist
society, recognising as equally valid the different national
traditions, does not seem to have been put forward seriously, for
the exclusion of the North-East, and the collapse of the Irish
Parliamentary Party in 1918, had left the Gaelic-inspired Sinn
Fein movement in a predominant position, providing after the
Civil War both the Government and the main opposition. In
this connection it is significant that in the new State at no period
did parties other than those derived directly from Sinn Fein,
hold more than a small minority of seats in the Dail, and with
the single exception of the Labour Party, which ante-dated by
almost a decade the foundation of the State and has survived the
whole half-century of independence, none of these parties lasted
for any longer than a few years. Moreover only one or two of
these nine evanescent groups could fairly be said to have represented a viewpoint clearly distinct from that of Sinn Fein and
its successor parties.

The provisions by which the Irish language was made essential for employment purposes in the public services and for
public examinations, were paralleled by other more intangible,
but none the less psychologically important changes which
helped to elevate one particular tradition to a unique place in
the new State. The teaching of modern Irish history in most
schools took on a new dimension—the 'physical force' movement that culminated in 1916 being glorified, while the constitutional 'Home Rule' approach was played down, and the
unionist tradition excoriated. Moreover through its public
commemorations the new State emphasised its origins in the
Sinn Fein movement, and those who did not belong to this
tradition were given some reason to feel they did not fully
belong to the new society being created.

The fact that the official Irish culture was thus narrowed to
a part of the Irish tradition which, despite its obvious importance, represented only one of several strands in the country's
cultural inheritance, had important effects on the sense of
security and identity of its inhabitants. Because only a minority
felt at home speaking or writing Irish, even after a full generation of the revival movement, most people in the new State
became in some measure culturally schizophrenic. A sense of
inadequacy and guilt surrounded their only partly successful
efforts to acquire a command of Irish, while their enjoyment of

the culture available to them in their home language, English, was marred by a feeling that even Anglo-Irish literature was in some way alien. Moreover, with few exceptions—of whom Sean O'Riada was one—Irish artists, musicians and writers failed to transmute their inheritance of folk music, stories, crafts and traditions into works of art valid for a modern European society of the twentieth century. Finally, the openness of an English-speaking society to Anglo-American influences, especially at a time when mass communications were coming into their own, weakened the national sense of identity. Against this background it is, perhaps, not surprising that the debate on EEC membership in the Republic was marked by a sense of uncertainty on this issue of cultural identity—although the polyglot cultures of the Continental members of the Community would not appear likely to have much direct impact on Irish culture, either in Irish or in English.

Doubts about cultural identity amongst Northern Ireland Protestants thus find something of a parallel amongst Catholics in the Republic. The turbulent history of Ireland, with its incomplete colonisation, intrusion of a religious division into the Irish scene, and imposition of the English language on a people with a most ancient Gaelic tradition, has had profoundly disturbing psychological effects in both parts of Ireland, and poses very great problems indeed for those who might seek to encourage the emergence of an all-Irish culture, comprehending so many diverse strands, and satisfying the deep aspirations of so many widely different groups of people sharing the complex common heritage of their land.

Divisive Effects of Growth of Catholic Influence in The Republic

The creation of a new neo-Gaelic orthodoxy to which all in the new independent Irish State were expected to subscribe was accompanied, from the latter part of the 1920s onwards, by the elevation of the Catholic Church in practice to a special position in the new State. In no respect was the small Protestant minority discriminated against; indeed successive governments leant over backwards to avoid any such discrimination, and in certain aspects, such as in the composition of the original, nominated, Senate and later, in the provision of aid for Protestant education, they effectively discriminated in favour of this minority. Moreover in the early years of the new State there

were some indications of a desire on the part of the Cumann na
Gaedheal Government to reduce ecclesiastical influence. As
Dr. John Whyte points out, in his *Church and State in Modern
Ireland*,[1] bishops were not given representation in the Senate
of the Irish Free State, although provision had been made for
four Catholic bishops and two Church of Ireland bishops in the
Senate proposed in the last British Home Rule Bill of 1920.
Moreover, the new Government also tightened State control
over the educational system, and changed the financial regu-
lations governing the educational system in such a way as to
oblige schools run by religious orders to employ a proportion of
lay staff.

One of the first indications of a growing Roman Catholic
influence in the new state was provided by the divorce controversy of 1925. Fifty years ago the Irish Courts exercised no
jurisdiction in divorce *a vinculo*, for the Matrimonial Causes
Act, 1857, was not extended to Ireland, and Irish people seeking
a dissolution of marriage had to proceed by promoting a
Private Bill in the United Kingdom Parliament. (Such Bills
had been introduced in the pre-Union Irish Parliament.) This
position was subsequently modified in Northern Ireland by the
introduction in 1939 of legislation permitting the Courts to
grant divorce decrees on certain grounds.

In the part of Ireland that gained its independence, however,
it became clear at an early stage that although the Constitution
of 1922 placed no barrier in the way of divorce *a vinculo* it would
not be permitted by the legislature. The matter arose at an
early stage, in 1924, when three Private Bills for divorce were
lodged with the Examiner of Private Bills, in accordance with
the practice inherited from the Westminster Parliament. The
Joint Committee on Standing Orders, comprised of representatives of Dail and Senate, reported to both Houses that they
considered the position under Standing Orders unsatisfactory
as it gave unrestricted power to introduce Divorce Bills even in
cases where a judgment of a court of law (a divorce decree *a
mensa et thoro*, commonly referred to as a legal separation), had
not previously been secured—as had been the normal practice
prior to independence. Early in 1925, a Government motion in
the Dail proposed alterations in Standing Orders that would
have prevented a Bill of Divorce from being introduced, a pro-

[1] John Whyte, *Church and State in Modern Ireland*, pp. 34 and 35, Gill &
Macmillan, 1971.

cedure which, however, was ruled out of order in the Senate, on the grounds that the Private Bill procedure was a legal right which under Article 73 of the Constitution could be repealed or amended only by legislation. In June 1925, a motion was debated in the Senate which would have resolved this difficulty by requiring that Private Bills of Divorce would have to have a first reading before they could be further proceeded with—the assumption being that all such Bills would in practice be rejected. This was the occasion of the famous speech by W. B. Yeats, then a Senator, in which he proclaimed that the Protestant minority were 'no petty people'. Unfortunately, the speech contained such hostile references to Catholicism and the authenticity of the Gospels, that, in the words of the then Clerk of the Senate, Dr. Donal O'Sullivan,[2] 'it poisoned the atmosphere that surrounded the question of divorce'. The clash between the two Houses on the constitutional issue was never resolved, the three Bills were withdrawn, and there the matter rested until the enactment of the 1937 Constitution.

In the later 1920s there was further evidence of a revival of ecclesiastical influence. Dr. Whyte believes this may in part have been attributable to the fact that with the entry of the bulk of the Republicans into the Dail as the Fianna Fail party, the Government no longer felt secure in the backing of the Catholic ecclesiastical authorities, but he points out that with the exception of one Minister, whose austere Ulster outlook fitted in with the Catholic puritanism of his colleagues, all the other members of the Cumann na Gaedheal government were Catholics who in matters of public morality were probably just as ready as any bishop to see that traditional standards were maintained. This had been evident since the foundation of the State in legislation to censor films and to cut back the opening hours of public houses, as well as in the government motion to prevent the introduction of private divorce bills. But in 1929 legislation was introduced of a more controversial nature, providing for censorship of publications that were in their general tendency indecent or obscene, or which advocated birth-control. (Up to that time the law had coped with this problem by police prosecutions against indecent or obscene literature on display or sold to the public.)

The first Censorship Board comprised a Protestant, three

[2] *The Irish Free State and its Senate*, by Donal O'Sullivan, Faber & Faber, 1940, pp. 167-8.

Catholic laymen, and a Catholic priest—the latter being chairman. At one time or another, it banned most of the leading Irish writers of the time, as well as authors such as Sartre, Hemingway, Steinbeck, Tennessee Williams, and Graham Greene. Kate O'Brien's *Without my Cloak* was banned because of a single delicate reference to the fact that one of the characters, a nun, had in her youth, discovered her father in a homosexual relationship. This record together with the fact that a priest was Chairman, and perhaps even the very concept of 'censorship', made the Board's activities an object of adverse comment in Northern Ireland, although attitudes to sexual explicitness were probably not very different North and South. The reform of the Board in 1957, and changes in the law in 1967, which automatically 'un-ban' publications found to be indecent or obscene unless the ban is specifically re-imposed, have eliminated most of the practical objections to the system, but it remains a bone of contention to Northerners, although the fact that most of them probably share the code of sexual morals of the Republic and that the similar concept of film censorship (albeit with somewhat different standards), is accepted apparently without question in Northern Ireland, suggests that the Northern antipathy to censorship of publications owes a good deal to the simple fact that the Republic chose to tackle this problem in this way![3]

An element of competition for the conservative Catholic vote also seemed to have crept into Irish politics around this time. During the Civil War, Republicans who were Catholics—the vast majority—had been condemned and excommunicated by the Catholic hierarchy, and the Republicans who in 1926 founded Fianna Fail may have felt obliged to work their passage back to orthodoxy. One of the new party's leaders claimed in 1929 that they represented 'the big element of Catholicity'; and some Fianna Fail propaganda against the Government took the form of accusing it of being supported by the Freemasons— the Masonic Order being an important force amongst Irish Protestants. Fianna Fail officially supported the Censorship of Publications Bill, criticised the Government for failing to consult with the Catholic Hierarchy about the opening of diplomatic relations with the Vatican, and got in first with a Legi-

[3] For a full account of the Censorship of Publications in the Republic, see Michael Adams, *Censorship: The Irish Experience*, Scepter Books, Dublin, 1968.

timacy Bill to meet the wishes of the Hierarchy. Most striking of all, however, was Fianna Fail's (and incidentally the Labour Party's) support for Mayo County Council's action in refusing to appoint a librarian selected by the Local Appointments Commission, on the grounds that the woman in question was a Protestant. In the debate on this matter, Mr. DeValera also asserted that a Protestant ought not to be appointed a dispensary doctor in the mainly Catholic area.[4]

Against this background it was not surprising perhaps that the advent to power of Fianna Fail in 1932 inaugurated a period in which ecclesiastical influence reached its peak. In addition to public utterances which sought to identify 'Irish' with 'Catholic', further legislation was introduced to align the civil law with Catholic teaching. In retrospect the most significant piece of legislation of this kind was the inclusion in the Criminal Law Amendment Act, 1935, of a prohibition of the importation or sale of contraceptives. In conjunction with the Customs Consolidation Act, 1876, this 1935 legislation even had the effect of prohibiting the importation of contraceptives for personal use. This introduced a very serious divergence between the law North and South—and one which, as the years have passed, has assumed increasing practical importance. The fact that the Protestant Churches do not share the Catholic Church's views on this matter and that access to contraception has become widely accepted as a human right in other countries has made this divergence of law a major issue between the two parts of the country.

In 1971 this issue became a major source of public controversy within the Republic, which was heightened by an attempt by independent University senators to introduce a private members bill that would liberalise the position. Public opinion was deeply divided on the issue. Churchmen intervened in the debate, seeking to head off any change in the law. The most extreme opposition came from the Catholic Archbishop of Dublin, Dr. J. C. McQuaid, who ended a strongly-worded statement by warning that if politicians changed the law, this would bring a curse upon the country. The Cardinal Archbishop of Armagh, Dr. Conway, expressed his opposition in more diplomatic terms, seeking to mobilise public opinion against a change in the law rather than to impose an ecclesasitical viewpoint.

[4] Dail Debates, Vol. 39, Col. 517, 17/2/1931.

The question of the relationship with Northern Ireland was raised in the course of this controversy. Those who opposed change argued that the decision should be taken on its own merits, and that the question of the Republic's relationship with Northern Ireland was irrelevant at that time, and need not be considered until and unless the reunion of the country became a live issue. They added that contraception was against the natural law and encouraged immorality amongst the young, and that its legalisation in the Republic would lead inevitably to pressure for the legalisation of divorce and abortion. To the argument that free access to contraceptives had not debauched the Catholic people of Northern Ireland, as it was alleged it would do in the Republic, it was countered that this reflected a very special situation in the North, where the tension between the two religious communities ensured a high standard of fidelity amongst Catholics to the moral standards of their religion. This remarkable tribute to an allegedly beneficial moral effect of sectarianism was also accompanied by another argument, not readily reconcilable with the fears of a moral collapse in the Republic if the law were changed—one to the effect that the whole issue was a non-problem as anyone who wanted contraceptives could get them readily from Northern Ireland!

If the arguments in favour of retaining the law were somewhat self-contradictory, and not very convincing, they at any rate had the effect of causing the Government to pull back on this issue, despite earlier hints by the Taoiseach, Mr. Lynch, and the Minister for External Affairs, Dr. Hillery, that some change would be made in the law. The introduction of the Private Members' Bill in the Senate was first delayed and then defeated by the Government, as was a similar Bill in the Dail in February, 1972. The Government indicated, however, its intention of taking some action on the matter of some time in the future.

That opinion on this issue is very divided in the Republic is evident from a public opinion poll taken in May, 1971, which showed that 34% of those sampled favoured a change in the law, 63% were against and 3% had no opinion. There was a striking divergence of opinion amongst those over and under 35. Of the former, 72½% were against, 25% in favour and 2½% had no opinion, whereas of the younger element of the adult population 53% were for a change, 43% were against, and 4% had no view. The wording of the question was, unfortunately, rather general; had it been more specific and limited, referring not to 'the sale of contraceptives' but rather to the making of some change in the law to modify the existing total ban, the proportion in favour would certainly have been considerably higher. It is also of interest to note that this matter was very fully debated at the May, 1971, Ard-Fheis (Conference) of the Opposition Fine Gael party, which draws more of its support from the more conservative rural areas than do the other two parties, and that although no vote was taken observers estimated that the meeting was about evenly divided on the issue, and that a year later the Ard-Fheis voted for change.

In these circumstances, and in view of the sensitivity of this issue for opinion in Northern Ireland, and the support of the leaders of the Protestant Churches for a change in the law, it seems likely that such a change will be effected before long, possibly in the context of a development of the Republic's Northern Policy, and possibly involving the retention of some controls designed to limit access to contraception by young unmarried people.

The period which saw the introduction of the legal ban on contraception culminated in the preparation by the Government and adoption by the people of a new Constitution which in Dr. Whyte's words[5] was 'obviously marked by Catholic thought'. This is evident in articles dealing with the Family and Marriage (a constitutional bar on the dissolution of marriage was introduced, which, of course, had been absent from the 1922 Constitution), Education, Private Property and Religion. While the new Constitution maintained the guarantees of religious equality and non-discrimination that had been a feature of the 1922 Constitution, these provisions were preceded by a new section by which 'The State recognises the special position of the Holy Catholic Apostolic and Roman Church as the guardian of the Faith professed by the great majority of the citizens. The State also recognises the Church of Ireland, the Presbyterian Church in Ireland, the Methodist Church in Ireland, and the Religious Society of Friends in Ireland, as well as the Jewish congregations and other religious denominations existing in Ireland at the date of the coming into operation of the Constitution' (Article 44.1.10 and 20). Mr. DeValera defended this innovation in the Dail by saying that it

[5] *op. cit.* p. 51.

simply recognised a sociological fact and that 'if we are going to have a democratic State it is clear their whole philosophy of life is going to affect that, and that has to be borne in mind and the recognition of it is important'.[6] A generation later the inclusion of this provision recognising the special position of the Roman Catholic Church found only one defender in the Dail, a Labour deputy, and its proposed deletion from the Constitution—yet to be effected—was greeted by Cardinal Conway with the statement that its deletion would not cause him to shed any tears.

This Constitution (Article 41.3.2) also provided that 'no law shall be enacted providing for the grant of a dissolution of marriage', which is unambiguous. The same cannot be said for the following subsection, however: 'No person whose marriage has been dissolved under civil law of any other State but is a subsisting valid marriage under the law for the time being in force within the jurisdiction of the Government and Parliament established by this Constitution shall be capable of contracting a valid marriage within that jurisdiction during the lifetime of the other party to the marriage so dissolved.' In an important case in 1958[7] which was decided by the Supreme Court, contrary views were expressed by the judges on the significance of this subsection. (These views, however, not being the subject of successful arguments, do not offer any conclusive interpretation.) One judge thought that the subsection barred absolutely the re-marriage in Ireland of persons divorced elsewhere while another judge considered that it would have this effect only if legislation were first enacted to invalidate divorces granted outside Ireland—which has not in fact happened.[8] However, on legal advice the Department of Social Welfare treats wives divorced in Britain by husbands domiciled there as being no longer married.[9]

This matter was considered by a parliamentary Committee on the Constitution, which reported in December, 1967. The Committee, whose report was unanimous, but did not bind the parties to which its members belonged, said that Article 41.3.2

[6] Dail Debates LXVII, 1890, June 4, 1937.

[7] *Mayo Perrott* v. *Mayo Perrott*, 1958—Irish Reports 336.

[8] For a discussion of this case and of the law on divorce see Prof. John M. Kelly, *Fundamental Rights in Irish Law*, Allen Figgis, Dublin, 1961, pp. 147–150.

[9] Dail Debates, Vol. 257, No. 1, 23/11/1971, Cols. 31–32 and Vol. 258 No. 12, 15/2/1972, Cols. 1703–1706.

had been criticised on the grounds that it took no heed of the wishes of a certain minority of the population; that it was also argued that the Constitution was intended for the whole of Ireland in which the proportion of Roman Catholics, though large, is not overwhelming; that the prohibition was a source of embarrassment to those seeking to bring about better relations between North and South; that there were other predominantly Catholic countries which did not in their Constitutions absolutely prohibit divorce; and that a more liberal attitude now prevailed in Catholic circles in regard to the rites and practices of other religious denominations, particularly since the Second Vatican Council. The Committee did not, however, conclude, as their reasoning might lead one to expect, that the provision should be deleted from the Constitution, but rather that it should be re-worded to preclude the granting of a dissolution of a religious marriage on grounds other than those acceptable to that religion.

This proposal was not well received. Some Protestant churchmen took it as suggesting that their denominations accepted divorce, and rejected this suggestion vigorously; Cardinal Conway and other members of the Roman Catholic Hierarchy denounced it in emphatic terms; and liberal opinion was unenthusiastic about a proposal that would introduce into the law of Ireland distinctions between people of different religious denominations.

This committee also proposed the deletion of Article 41.3.3, because of its ambiguity, leaving the recognition of foreign divorces to be determined in accordance with private international law, 'the principles of which have been fairly well established'.

No action has since been taken on this matter. While there is general recognition that the present state of the law is unsatisfactory, involving ambiguity and potential clashes between the civil law and both private international law and ecclesiastical law, and while many of these difficulties could be remedied by simply deleting these constitutional provisions, without introducing divorce into the Irish legal system, there has been a political reluctance to grasp this nettle, owing to the risks attaching to a step which could be misinterpreted as a step towards the introduction of divorce legislation. The experience of politicians in connection with the controversy on contraception in 1971 has tended to confirm this reluctance. Nevertheless privately many politicians accept the need for a clarification of the law through some amendment to the Constitution, and especially, in the context of North/South relations, for the deletion of the ban on divorce in the Constitution, and such changes might be effected in conjunction with other constitutional reforms, especially if they were put forward as being necessary to make the Constitution more acceptable to Northern opinion.

On the actual introduction of divorce in the Republic, political attitudes are much harder. Support for divorce is very much a minority view, although the minority is not insignificant. A public opinion poll in May, 1971, showed 22% favouring its introduction, 73% against and 5% undecided. Amongst the under-34 age group, support was much stronger—34% in favour and $61\frac{1}{2}$% against, and $4\frac{1}{2}$% undecided.[10] Moreover divergences between the *legal* (as distinct from constitutional) provisions with respect to divorce in Northern Ireland and the Republic are not, perhaps, quite as sensitive an issue in North-South relations as contraception. The existence of different divorce provisions even within a unitary State is not unknown— thus within the United Kingdom there are different divorce laws in England and Wales, Scotland and Northern Ireland, and such provisions are normal in federal states. If there had been pressure from the Protestant minority for divorce as a civil right, and if this had been resisted by the Government and parliament, the position would be somewhat different, but this is not the case, although the attitude of the ecclesiastical authorities of some Protestant denominations towards divorce may no longer be as hostile as was indicated at the time of the publication of the Report of the Constitution Committee in 1967.

None of the legislative measures introduced in the 1920s and 1930s, and none of the provisions of the 1937 Constitution involved direct discrimination against Protestants, and the actual hardship imposed on Protestants—or Catholics—who found the censorship of publications or the ban on contraception unacceptable was, perhaps, not very great, as the laws could usually be evaded without much risk of prosecution. But even Protestants interested neither in banned books nor in contraception could scarcely feel at home in a society in which laws on such matters were devised and enacted in accordance

[10] *This Week*, June 25, 1971.

with the particular views of the Roman Catholic Church, and without regard for Protestant attitudes.

This process continued after the introduction of the new Constitution in 1937, although for a period the centre of gravity shifted away from issues of public morality or constitutional law towards special issues. Moreover, the Fianna Fail Party, in office for sixteen years after 1932, became less clerically-orientated and during the 1940s was prepared to face conflict with the Roman Catholic Hierarchy on certain issues. The dominant event in Church-State relations during this period was undoubtedly the Mother and Child Health Scheme controversy of 1951, which made a powerful and lasting impact on Protestant opinion north of the border. The fact that a social welfare scheme was withdrawn by a government following objections by the Roman Catholic Hierarchy, whose opinion on it had been sought by that government, and that the full light of publicity was cast on these events through the resignation of the Minister responsible for the scheme, Dr. Noel Browne, and the publication by him of the relevant documents, made this a *cause célèbre*. Arguably it was a Pyrrhic victory for the Roman Catholic Hierarchy for the scheme was subsequently introduced with certain modifications and, more important, the publicity attaching to this matter and the reaction of public opinion in Northern Ireland and outside Ireland, must have made it difficult for the Hierarchy to adopt such a clear-cut attitude on other issues in the years that followed. It is also fair to add that because it was the intervention of the Catholic Hierarchy that was seen to stop this project in its tracks, the fact was obscured that the proposed legislation had features which might be judged objectionable even by those not committed to a particular and very conservative view of Catholic social teaching which to-day commands little support within the Church. But these considerations are unimportant beside the impact which this controversy made on opinion in Northern Ireland where it appeared to confirm a widespread belief amongst Protestants that the government of the Republic is under the effective control of the Roman Catholic Hierarchy.

Since the Mother and Child Scheme controversy in 1951 there have been relatively few cases where the influence of the Roman Catholic Hierarchy on legislation has given rise to controversy, although in the lee of the Mother and Child Scheme, legislation for legal adoption was enacted by Fianna Fail which contained provisions still in effect which make it impossible for a married couple who differ in religion to adopt a child. The Government is considering an amendment to this law.

More significant, because it has happened in the midst of the Northern crisis, was the proposal by the Minister for Education in 1971—made without consultation with the Protestant authorities—for a post-primary school rationalisation system that would have involved the merger of multi-denominational local authority schools with Roman Catholic secondary schools in new 'Community' schools to be vested in trustees to be appointed by the Roman Catholic bishop, and to be managed by committees two-thirds of whose members would be appointed by the Roman Catholic secondary school authorities. In formulating this proposal, which is further discussed in the next chapter (and which, it must be said, was later radically modified), the Minister was under a misapprehension as to the interest of the Protestant community in the multi-denominational vocational schools, many of which counted few or no Protestant pupils on their rolls, but the Minister's proposal was nevertheless indicative of an attitude of mind that can scarcely commend itself to Protestants. Moreover, the fact that this proposal was put forward at a time when there was much public and parliamentary discussion about the need to create in the Republic a pluralist society of a kind that could be acceptable to Northern Protestant also suggests a high degree of insensitivity to this crucial issue at both civil service and ministerial level.

The attitude of the Protestant community in the Republic to these events has throughout almost the whole history of the independent Irish State been rather passive. Despite the very large representation they were given in the original nominated Senate—which gradually diminished during the 1920s and early 1930s as the seats in the Senate were filled by election rather than nomination—the members of the Protestant minority tended from the beginning to opt out of public life and to confine themselves to their professional and business activities. Their representation in the Dail, while at times more than proportional to their share of the total population and electorate, has never been proportional to their strength amongst the groups in the population from which most Dail deputies have been drawn—viz. larger farmers, businessmen and professional people. To a considerable degree, therefore, those members of the Protestant minority who did not in fact emigrate after the State was founded but remained in the country, can be said to have opted out of the running of the new State. This reaction was, perhaps, an understandable one from such a small minority, which must have found the political atmosphere of the new regime somewhat distasteful, and must also have felt itself too weak in numbers to exercise much influence on the evolution of the State. If the minority had suffered any overt discrimination, they might have been provoked to take political action to protect their interests, but from the start the new State avoided anything of the kind, and to many Protestants it may, therefore, have seemed best to lie low and say nothing, ignoring the indirect, and in practice not very important, impact on them of the kind of legislation just referred to. The contrast between pre-independence fears of intolerance or discrimination in an independent Ireland with a Roman Catholic majority and the way in which the minority found itself treated in the new State, must have encouraged sighs of relief and a feeling that Providence should not be tempted by complaining about the unintended effects of occasional unconsciously Catholic-orientated legislation or about certain aspects of the 1937 Constitution.

It is only at the very end of the period, in connection with controversies arising from liberal Catholic efforts to have the law on contraception amended, and in connection with the community schools controversy, where Catholics were in fact first to protest against the ignoring of Protestant interests, that authoritative Protestant voices have belatedly been raised in protest against provisions which, however unintentionally, have adverse implications for the Protestant community.

Seen from the viewpoint of Northern Protestants, the situation of their co-religionists in the Republic has appeared less than ideal. Although fair-minded members of the Northern Protestant community would admit that the condition of Protestants in the Republic has contrasted very favourably with that of Catholics in the North, this does not mean that they see it as satisfactory. The absence of vocal protests from the Protestant minority in the Republic, which might appear to indicate that their condition is not too unfavourable, does not convince the average Northern Protestant that all is well. He is inclined rather to regard his Southern co-religionist as having been cowed into silence about what from a Northern viewpoint appear as legitimate grievances, and this itself is often taken as evidence that the conditions under which Protestants live in the Republic are less than satisfactory. To put matters at their best, while there may not be much about life in the Republic to worry seriously a fair-minded Northern Protestant, there is equally little to attract him; to exchange membership of a society in which he enjoys a predominant and even privileged position, for participation in a community in which Gaelic nationalism and Roman Catholicism appear as dominant cultural forces, seems to him a poor proposition, and the absence of actual discrimination against Protestants is a somewhat negative counter-selling point.

Moreover, to the Northern Protestant, the numerical decline of the Protestant community in the Republic is a source of concern; the reasons for this decline are not understood, but the mere fact of the decline is sufficient for many Northern Protestants to conclude simplistically that re-unification would lead to a similar drop in their numbers, although a detailed study of the causes of the disparity in the trends of the Protestant population North and South of the Border does not support this thesis.

The striking character of the disparity in Protestant population trends in the two parts of Ireland is best illustrated by one simple comparison: between 1926 and 1961 the Protestant population of Northern Ireland increased by 92,000, or 11%; that of the Republic fell by 76,000, or 35%.

Dr. Brendan Walsh of the Economic and Social Research Institute has sought an explanation of this trend in a paper published by that body.[11] His study shows that in 1960/62 the age-specific fertility of Protestant marriages was actually somewhat higher in the Republic than in Northern Ireland (Table 2B), but as a result of the less favourable age pattern of the Protestant community in the Republic the actual number of births per 1,000 Protestant married women aged 15–44 was somewhat higher in Northern Ireland. He also shows that Protestants have a higher marriage rate in Northern Ireland than in the Republic, and suggests that this may be 'a reflection of the very small size of the (Protestant) community in the Republic, combined with a desire to avoid inter-marriage'.

The combined effects of the less favourable age pattern and lower marriage rate of Protestants in the Republic, offsetting somewhat higher fertility, is a lower Protestant birth rate in the

[11] Brendan M. Walsh, 'Religion and Demographic Behaviour in Ireland', ESRI Paper No. 55, May, 1970.

Republic. However, the differential between Protestant birth rates in the Republic and in Northern Ireland is much too large, in Dr. Walsh's view, to be accounted for by these factors alone. He notes that Census of Population data shows a higher proportion of Protestants than Catholics in the Republic to be married (about 10% more) and concludes that the marriage statistics, which show a 40% higher annual marriage rate for Catholic than Protestant men, and a 25% higher annual marriage rate for Catholic than Protestant women, must be distorted by mixed marriages, virtually all of them in Catholic churches. On the assumption that the true marriage rates for the two denominations are similar (in view of the higher proportion of Protestants who are married this may be a conservative assumption) he calculates that almost 30% of Protestant men and 20% of Protestant women in the Republic married Catholics in 1961.

In view of the way in which the *Ne Temere* decree and more recent legislation of the Catholic Church operate to require the children of such marriages to be brought up as Catholics, this implies a 'leakage' of perhaps 25% per generation from the Protestant community in the Republic. In Northern Ireland, by contrast, the division between the two communities has been so intense, and the social contacts between them so minimal, that no equivalent force has operated to erode the Protestant community there.

Finally, Dr. Walsh points out that the Protestant community in the Republic is a much older community than in Northern Ireland. In 1961 17% of Protestants in the Republic were aged 65 or over as against less than 11% in Northern Ireland. The death rate of Protestants in the Republic is correspondingly high—40% higher than that of the Catholic community over the period from 1946 to 1961.

Thus the decline of the Protestant community in the Republic is the result of the operation of a combination of forces—the fact that it is an older community, with a higher death rate and a lower proportion of women of child-bearing age; its lower marriage rate, which perhaps reflects the very small size of the Protestant community in the Republic; the consequent physical isolation of many Protestants vis-à-vis their co-religionists and fear of inter-marriage; and finally the high proportion of mixed marriages, and consequent 'leakage' as a result of the Catholic upbringing of the children of such marriages. It is clear from Dr. Walsh's paper that the decline of the Protestant community in the Republic is *not* due to emigration—its emigration rate from 1946 to 1961 was in fact 40% *lower* than that of the Catholic population.

It is clear from this that the fears of the Northern Protestant community that in a united Ireland their numbers would dwindle like those of the Protestants in the Republic have no foundation except to the extent that within a united Ireland closer social relations between the two communities in Northern Ireland, on the model of the Republic, would lead to an erosion of the Northern Protestant community through mixed marriages. It is a possible improvement in social relations between the two communities in Northern Ireland that creates the real danger to Protestant survival in the North—and the sad lesson of these figures for Northern Protestants is not that they should resist re-unification, but rather that they should keep the two communities in Northern Ireland as far apart as possible so long as the Catholic Church requires the children of mixed marriages to be brought up as Catholics, 'No fraternisation', rather than 'no surrender' on the Border issue, should logically be the Northern Protestant stance!

This conclusion raises a very serious issue for the Catholic Church; in conditions in which the continuance of the requirement to bring up all the children of all mixed marriages as Catholics puts a premium on the maintenance of a segregation between the two communities in Northern Ireland that has led to a polarisation which may even threaten the massacre or expulsion of the Catholic population of that province, can this policy be justified? That this provision is not an immutable law of the Catholic Church is evident from the fact that it was applied in Ireland only after the turn of the present century, when an older tradition, that the boys be brought up in the religion of their father and the girls in that of their mother, was abandoned following the technical promulgation of the relevant decree of the Council of Trent in Ireland and in certain other countries where it had not up till then been operative.[12] This question is pursued further in Chapter 9.

[12] The author's family tradition relates that in the middle of the last century a relative who contracted a mixed marriage gave birth to five boys and five girls. On Sundays the couple drove to church in Castleisland, Co. Kerry, the father taking the five boys to the Protestant church after leaving the mother and the five daughters to the Catholic church!

The strengthening of Roman Catholic influence in the Republic has been a product of Partition. The numerical weakness of the Protestant minority, and its somewhat passive acceptance of a measure of 'catholicization' of the independent Irish State, encouraged a trend which would most certainly have been strongly resisted by over a million Protestants in a united Ireland. It may be questioned whether the government of a united Ireland would ever have attempted to introduce legislation banning contraception or establishing a censorship of books, or whether it would have attempted to introduce a constitutional provision banning divorce with the right of remarriage. But even if such a government had attempted any of these things, they would certainly have been fiercely fought by the Protestant quarter of the population of a united Ireland.

No one can say what kind of relationship would have existed in a united Ireland between the Catholic majority and the Protestant minority; it does not necessarily follow that because the tiny Protestant minority in a truncated 26-county Irish State was not actively discriminated against by specifically sectarian legislation, no problem of intolerance would have arisen in a united Ireland with a 25% Protestant minority. At the same time there is no Southern tradition of religious intolerance of the intensity of that which had existed in Northern Ireland for centuries.

That this is so is not, of course, necessarily proof of the existence of more angelic qualities amongst inhabitants of the Republic, Catholic and Protestant, than amongst the inhabitants of Northern Ireland. History placed two large communities of Catholic and Protestant small farmers and workers side by side in the countryside, towns and cities of Northern Ireland —two groups competing for scarce resources of land and employment. This was the consequence of a colonisation at once extensive and incomplete. Nothing similar happened in the territory of the Republic, save in parts of its three Ulster counties.[13] Thus throughout the greater part of the Republic the religious conflict was carried on *between* classes rather than *within* classes—and eventually the Protestant landlord class was defeated in the Land War, and ceased to be a significant economic force as a result of the subsequent land reforms, although

[13] The existence of a significant Protestant working class in Dublin led to sectarian conflicts in the city in the eighteenth century but these died out in the last century in circumstances which might repay study.

during the Civil War of 1922/23, there was a brief outburst of rural sectarianism in some parts of the country; houses owned by Protestants were burnt, and many Protestants left the country in this period.

This very different historical background goes a long way to explain the relative absence of sectarianism or bigotry in the Republic. The fact that within its territory the Protestant community is so small—a mere 5%—as to constitute no threat to the majority has certainly contributed to this happier state of affairs, and goes a long way towards explaining the success of the independent Irish State in establishing good relations between the two religious communities.

But whatever a united Ireland would have been like in terms of the relationship between the two religious communities, it is safe to say that this relationship would have been very different from that which has in fact existed within the 26-county Irish State. Here as elsewhere Partition created a new and different pattern—one which has tended to some degree to be self-perpetuating as the growing Roman Catholic influence in the Republic has with the passing of time made the prospect of reunion less attractive to Northern Protestants.

3. Effects in the North

The most significant changes resulting from Partition, and having the effect of dividing more deeply North from South, have probably been those occurring in the Republic, where the achievement of independence naturally led to some adjustments to the system of government and the laws that had prevailed when the whole of Ireland had been within the United Kingdom. In Northern Ireland the emphasis lay on the retention of the status quo; the whole purpose of the exercise by Northern Ireland of its option to secede from the new Irish State was, of course, to retain its existing position within the United Kingdom.

Nevertheless even in an area ruled by a party as conservative as the Unionists, there have inevitably been changes different from those occurring in the Republic, and some of the widening of the gap between North and South since 1920 has thus been due to developments in Northern Ireland. Moreover the retention in Northern Ireland of antiquated laws or practices, e.g. the multiple 'business' vote, long after they had been replaced by more democratic processes both in Great Britain and the Republic, was a source of division also, although the reforms introduced since 1968 have removed these historical anomalies.

The principal changes that took place within the North, and which represented a fresh source of division between North and South, have been changes in the electoral system or in the pattern of public appointments or housing allocations designed to consolidate the power of the Unionist majority, and changes in the educational system. In the latter case the changes in the North have, however, in some instances at least, represented improvements not yet matched in the Republic, so that in these cases it has been the failure of the Republic to progress in this field at the same rate as Northern Ireland that has created a gap between practices in the two areas. In addition to these legislative or administrative changes in Northern Ireland, there has also been a widening of the cultural gap caused by the emergence in Northern Ireland of patterns of behaviour similar to those developing in the United Kingdom, but not paralleled, to the same degree at any event, in the Republic. Except in the matter of Sunday observance the growing permissiveness of society in the United Kingdom has thus been more fully reflected in Northern Ireland than in the Republic, making greater inroads on the Northern Protestant ethic than on the Southern Roman Catholic one.

The two parts of Ireland had started off with the same system for the election of their parliaments and their local authorities—viz. proportional representation in multi-seat constituencies with the single transferable vote. This system, never employed in Great Britain, had been introduced in Ireland immediately before the establishment of Northern Ireland and the foundation of an independent State in the remainder of Ireland. While the original impetus had come from a local demand in one Irish urban centre, Sligo, the willingness of the British Government to introduce it generally was no doubt influenced by the manner in which in 1918 the 'X' voting system in single-seat constituencies had produced in Ireland as a whole an overwhelming majority of seats (70%) for Sinn Fein candidates, who had secured only 47% of the popular vote in that election. This result must have brought home to British politicians the extent to which the effective working of their antiquated voting system—the placing of a mark opposite a single name is the most simplified electoral system possible, inherited from the pre-literate era—depended upon special features of political geography in Britain. (In the first quarter of this century, with the extension of universal suffrage, this system was abandoned throughout Continental Europe and survived principally in the United States and certain 'white' Dominions such as Canada and Australia which were organised on a federal basis with strongly marked geographical differences in political allegiance similar to those existing in Great Britain; these ensure the survival of a substantial opposition in parliament even in the face of significant swings in electoral support.)

But although before introducing the Government of Ireland

Act, 1920, upon which the government of Northern Ireland—but not of the Republic[1]—has since been based, the British Government replaced the 'X' voting system in single-seat constituencies by proportional representation in multi-seat constituencies for both local government purposes and for the election of members to the two Irish Parliaments, they did not take any steps to prevent the Northern Ireland Government from abolishing this new system in favour of that which had previously existed, save for a provision in Section 14 of the Act, preventing such a change in respect of parliamentary elections for a period of three years. The new Northern Ireland Government at once, in 1921, reverted to the former electoral system for local government purposes, and made a similar change before its parliamentary elections in 1929. (The 'X' system in single-seat constituencies had, of course, been retained for the election of Northern Ireland members to the Westminster Parliament.)

The reasons for these changes are a matter for debate. In the case of the local authority elections, however, it is indisputable that the change of electoral system was followed by gerrymandering of electoral boundaries which secured for the Unionist Party majorities in several local authorities where the majority of voters were in fact anti-Unionist; because of the greater proliferation of boundaries capable of being adjusted for party purposes where there are a larger number of single-seat constituencies, the reversion to the 'X' system in single-seat constituencies for local election purposes certainly facilitated this gerrymandering. (This gerrymandering is well-documented in Frank Gallagher's *The Indivisible Island*[2]—an avowedly propagandist work but one which effectively displays some of the relevant facts and figures with appropriate maps.)

The abolition of proportional representation before Northern Ireland Parliamentary elections in 1929 does not appear to have been similarly directed against the anti-Unionist opposition. Professor McCracken[3] suggests that it was intended rather to deal with the danger of an erosion of official Unionist strength in the Northern Ireland Parliament as a result of the emergence

[1] So far as that part of Ireland now constituting the Republic is concerned, the provisions of this Act were replaced by the Anglo-Irish Treaty of 1921 and the Irish Free State Constitution of 1922, and subsequently by the Constitution of 1937.

[2] Frank Gallagher, *The Indivisible Island*, Victor Gollancz, London, 1957.

[3] Professor J. L. McCracken, 'The Political Scene in Northern Ireland 1926–1927' in *The Years of the Great Test*, Mercier Press, Cork, 1967.

of Unionist splinter groups—such as the Unbought Tenants, who in 1925 won a seat held by a Parliamentary Secretary, or the Local Optionists (temperance reformers seeking a measure of local option that would make possible more stringent liquor licensing laws in certain areas) who contested the 1929 General Election in certain constituencies. Paradoxically in the 1969 General Election it was the 'X' system in single-seat constituencies which helped the Unionist splinter groups, encouraging some official Unionists to reconsider the introduction of proportional representation. The reason for this change was that whereas in 1929 the danger to Unionist power came from splinter groups that commanded in certain areas a minority of the Unionist vote, and that might have secured representation under a proportional system, in 1969 a much more fundamental danger was the emergence of a Protestant Extremist movement which might secure in some areas a majority of the Unionist vote, but which might have been kept in a minority with the aid of lower preference votes of anti-Unionists, had proportoinal representation with the single transferable vote been in operation.

But whatever the motivation of these changes in the Northern Ireland Electoral system during the 1920s the abolition of proportional representation in Northern Ireland and the reversion to the 'X' system in single-seat constituencies, created a notable divergence between the two political systems North and South of the Border, more especially as this change permitted gerrymandering at least in local elections. This was facilitated by the permanently polarised political attitudes of a population which was in large measure geographically segregated—partly at least by choice—within local communities, and whose continued segregation could be secured by local Unionist control of housing allocations.

It cannot be said that the South has been free from a measure of gerrymandering also, but on a scale that has necessarily been much less significant. Local authority elections in rural areas in the Republic have continued to be based on long-established and politically-unbiassed local authority areas, and the unpolarised and unsegregated character of support for the parties has inhibited gerrymandering in urban areas where boundaries for local election purposes are more fluid. Moreover, the smaller number of boundaries to be 'fiddled' under conditions of proportional representation has made gerrymandering much more difficult in parliamentary elections, for which boundary changes are now required fairly frequently in order to fulfil a constitutional requirement for a very close proportionality between population and seats.

It is true that in 1969 the *number* of seats in constituencies were adjusted to the relative strengths of the political parties in these areas—thus gaining for the government party five or six extra seats in addition to the 69 or 70 which a more impartial system of constituency determination would have given them.[4]

The distortion thus created—the maximum possible within the proportional representation system as it existed in the Republic in 1969—was large enough in the context of the prevailing evenly-balanced political situation to change the outcome of that General Election, giving to Fianna Fail a majority it could not otherwise have achieved. Nevertheless this distortion was small by comparison with that possible—and frequently secured—under the 'X' voting system in single-seat constituencies in Northern Ireland, aided as it has been by the clear-cut geographical segregation of the majority and minority in many areas.

[4] Under this electoral system the proportion of seats in a constituency secured by a party with a given proportion of votes can vary according to the number of seats in the constituency. Thus a party with approximately 38–42% of the votes would normally secure one seat in a three-seat constituency (viz. $33\frac{1}{2}\%$), two seats in a four-seat constituency (50%), and two seats also in a five-seat constituency (40%). Thus by dividing a region in which it enjoyed the support of around 38–42% of the voters into four-seater constituencies a government would maximise its parliamentary support from this region. Similarly where its support is normally in excess of 45%, such a party could maximise its parliamentary representation with three-seat constituencies, in which it would in most cases secure two out of three seats ($66\frac{2}{3}\%$), with less than half the popular vote.

In 1969 the Fianna Fail Government re-drew the constituencies in such a way as to create four-seat constituencies throughout the Dublin region where it enjoyed the support of about 40% of the voters, and three-seat constituencies in most of rural Ireland, and especially in the West, where the party could count on receiving upwards of 45% of the first preference votes. As a result, although Fianna Fail's national share of first preference votes fell from 47.7% to 45.7% its share of seats rose from 50.0% to 52.1%. This virtually trebled from 2.3% to 6.4%, the 'bonus'—the margin by which, even where proportional representation is operated fairly, the largest party tends to secure a slightly larger share of seats than votes. Only once before—in 1943, when the opposition was fragmented and when almost 20% of the popular vote went to candidates not belonging to the three main parties—had a bonus of this magnitude ever been secured by the majority party at a General Election in the Republic.

The changes that were effected in the 1920s in the electoral system in Northern Ireland, combined with subsequent gerrymandering of electoral boundaries, for local election purposes at least,[5] introduced into Northern Ireland politics, on a scale that was not, and could not have been, paralleled in the Republic, an element of inequity and injustice to the minority that helped to reinforce its lack of respect for and acceptance of the regime—especially as the undemocratic Unionist control of a number of important local authorities in areas where the anti-Unionist population was in a majority, was used unscrupulously to deprive those politically opposed to Unionism of much of their entitlement to public housing, and to locate such public housing as was allocated to them in such a way geographically as to maintain indefinitely the unjust political balance thus secured. Some at least of the failure to secure from the minority acceptance of the authority of the Northern Ireland political system derived from these political changes effected in the 1920s which deprived the Northern Ireland Government of legitimate authority in the eyes of those who were thus discriminated against, both politically and in terms of social justice.

To some extent, of course, this discrimination ante-dated the establishment of Northern Ireland. Political patronage for certain public appointments was a feature of nineteenth-century Britain and Ireland, and is a phenomenon that survives for certain posts to this day. The problem of injustice which this poses is, however, felt more acutely when political alignments are fixed by considerations of religion, or race, or colour, which are pre-determined in each individual case. Moreover, legislation enacted in the independent Irish State shortly after independence not only firmly established the pre-independence system of merit appointments in the central government service, but also extended to it to local authority appointments. No such legislation was enacted at that time in Northern Ireland, and minority participation above the lowest levels in the local authority service in Northern Ireland as a result was minimal.

[5] Frank Gallagher (*op. cit.* pp. 234–238) claims that Derry City, and the counties of Tyrone and Fermanagh were gerrymandered in 1929 for the purpose of parliamentary elections but Barritt and Carter (*The Northern Ireland Problem*, Oxford University Press, 1962, p. 42) come to the conclusion that gerrymandering did not have 'any large influence on parliamentary, as opposed to local, elections'.

This problem has been belatedly tackled in the 1969 reform programme.

It is difficult to over-estimate the cumulative effects of an antiquated franchise; unjust electoral boundaries that gave control of certain local authorities to Unionist minorities in these areas; consequent discriminatory housing allocations, partly connected with the propping up of this gerrymander; and discrimination in public appointments at local authority level. Over fifty years these features of Northern Ireland life, combined with the automatic Unionist majority in parliament and the equally automatic minority position of the anti-Unionists in that assembly, had a profoundly alienating effect. This effect was all the more powerful because this half-century saw great changes in the rest of the world, so that by the end of the 1960s features of Northern Ireland life which were, perhaps, not so extraordinary in the context of the Europe of 1920, stuck out like sore thumbs. This was true for example of the multiple business vote; but it was true in a much more general way of the whole atmosphere of Northern Ireland, steeped in discrimination based most unhappily on religious divisions that had acquired a special political significance in this area.

Thus the acuteness of the alienation of the Northern minority to-day, while it owes something to new types of discrimination introduced after the establishment of Northern Ireland or to old types of discrimination intensified under local Unionist rule up to 1969, also owes a good deal to the growing unwillingness of the minority, conscious of a more liberal world outside the North, to accept at the end of the 1960s what they had resented but lived with in the 1920s. The very stagnation of the system in Northern Ireland in a context of a rapidly changing external environment, thus became paradoxically a dynamic force, making for radical changes by the end of this half-century.

But because the Republic was not experiencing the same kind of problems, this new and dynamic force for change in the North found no precise counterpart in that part of Ireland and some at least of the problems of North/South relations in the late 1960s reflected difficulties of comprehension not alone between the Northern Unionists and the Republic but also between the Northern minority, radicalised by their growing discontent, and the bulk of the population in the Republic, for whom Civil Rights at first had an alien, and even sinister left-wing ring. While some of these gaps in understanding were subsequently bridged, the very different experience of people North and South of the Border after 1968 has created fresh divergences in attitudes; the members of the Northern minority to-day have quite different attitudes on some issues from those of people in the Republic, who have not shared their experiences. If the island of Ireland were to be magically re-united tomorrow, these differences would be seen to be quite significant.

It should, perhaps, be added that proposed changes in the structure of local government in Northern Ireland, based on the MacRory Report, will introduce a new dimension of differentiation into the North/South relationship. Hitherto both North and South have maintained the local government structure inherited from the period of British rule—involving counties and county boroughs, with subordinate units such as urban districts. The only difference, indeed, has been that arising from the suppression of the subordinate rural district councils in the South some years after independence. But the reforms proposed for local government in Northern Ireland involve a completely new system, based on the hinterlands of various urban centres. The counties are abandoned as administrative units. In the Republic by contrast a local government reform proposed in a Government White Paper involves only relatively minor changes in the structure, and retains the counties as the primary units of local government. If both plans proceed, the difference in local government structure between North and South will within a few years have become very striking indeed.

CHANGES IN EDUCATIONAL SYSTEM

Although both parts of Ireland inherited the same educational system fifty years ago, changes have occurred, principally although not exclusively, in Northern Ireland, which, while not significantly altering the religious basis of the educational system, have created certain important differences.

At the very outset the two systems evolved in different directions. In Northern Ireland, the work formerly carried out by the Educational Commissioner was largely transferred to Local Education Authorities; in the Republic it was transferred to the Department of Education. Neither system worked very satisfactorily. In the North the new role of the Local Education

Authorities was never accepted by the Roman Catholic school or ecclesiastical authorities, partly because of the way in which many of the local authorities which appointed the Local Education Authorities were controlled by Unionists, some of them elected following a gerrymandering of constituency boundaries. In the Republic for forty years the Department of Education adopted a passive role, leading to general stagnation of the educational system and when it finally burst into activity in the first half of the 1960s, its bureaucratic and centralised character prevented it from securing for its reforms the support of many conservative educational interests.

The Local Education Authorities in the North were set up by a controversial Act of 1923, which gave to these Authorities the power to maintain schools transferred to them by their former managers, to build new ones where needed, and to appoint teachers. It also forbade these Authorities to provide any religious instruction, or to take religion into account in appointing teachers. There was no compulsion, however, on schools to transfer to the new system, which took little account of the desire of Roman Catholics and of many Protestants (Anglican rather than Presbyterian) to retain a denominational system, but schools which opted out of the new system (described as 'voluntary schools') could receive no building grant or grants for upkeep or equipment.

This system was modified in 1925 and again in 1930 to meet Protestant objections; Local Education Authorities were empowered to give religious instruction and teachers could be required to give Bible teaching, although no child could be compelled to attend. Moreover, the schools which transferred to this Local Education Authority system were to have representatives appointed by the Minister for Education on the Local Education Authorities (County Education Committees), and teachers would be appointed by School Management Committees, thus meeting Protestant objections to the possible appointment of Catholic teachers to Protestant schools which transferred. Finally, schools which did not transfer to the Local Education authority system were given 50% grants.

There the matter rested until the Butler Act in Britain in 1944 re-opened the whole question. There followed a Northern Ireland White Paper and legislation which established a new system of junior or secondary intermediate schools, providing a general course in fundamental subjects but concentrating rather on practical subjects, and senior secondary schools providing facilities for academically talented pupils, 80% of the places being awarded on an 11-plus test, and 20% by the schools themselves. Grants of 65% were offered to voluntary schools which agreed that their premises should not be used for unapproved purposes after schools hours, and which accepted one-third representation for the Local Education Authority on their management boards. Religious instruction in Local Education Authority schools was not to be distinctive of any religious denomination, and teachers were no longer to be compelled to give religious instruction. Finally, the system of appointment of teachers by School Management Committees, which had been introduced in 1930 to guarantee Protestants against the appointment of Catholics as teachers in Protestant schools transferred to the Local Education Authorities was modified, leading to a storm of protests from Protestants. This was largely responsible for the delay in enacting this legislation, which did not reach the statute book until 1947.

Subsequent legislation in 1950 created another kind of voluntary school—one which would not receive the 65% building grants but which would be paid a fixed amount in fees and would be free—which the schools receiving the 65% building grant were not—to use these State fees, in conjunction with any private fees they could secure, for building purposes.

Finally, in 1967, the problems created by a system that left the voluntary schools, Protestant and Catholic, with insufficient resources for expansion, was further modified by an Act which created a new category of 'maintained schools', which in return for accepting one-third representation from Local Education Authorities to be nominated by the Minister for Education—a provision hitherto resisted by most Catholic schools—would receive 80% capital grants. This was reluctantly accepted by the Roman Catholic Hierarchy in May, 1968, in return for a concession increasing the powers of School Management Committees vis-à-vis those of the Local Education Authorities.

Thus after many vicissitudes the principle of joint—although not equal—participation in management was accepted by the Catholic Church in Northern Ireland.

In the Republic, however, developments took a different shape. The only significant educational reform in the first forty years of independence was the introduction in 1930 of vocational schools, in theory and sometimes in practice multi-denominational, based on the former technical schools, and providing a form of education which approximated most nearly to secondary modern education in Britain. This school system, paralleling the voluntary secondary schools, is organised by Vocational Education Committees linked to local authorities.

No such link exists between the voluntary secondary schools and these Committees, however, and recent developments have pointed to a move away from the Local Authority system. As was mentioned in the preceding chapter, proposals were made by the Minister for Education in 1971 for a rationalisation of post-primary education in twenty-five centres throughout the country by a merger of publicly-owned vocational schools and private schools run by Catholic religious orders. The new schools were to be vested in trustees to be appointed by the local Catholic bishop, and to be managed by committees, two-thirds of whose members would be appointed by the private school owners, regardless of the relative size or number of the existing public or private schools in each area. This proposal met with a resounding set-back, first of all because of opposition from the religious orders owning and running the private schools, who were not prepared to accept even the one-third representation that the public vocational school interests would have had on the management committee or the transfer of ownership to trustees to be appointed by the local Catholic bishop. Subsequently the Minister went ahead with a similar proposal in two new and rapidly-expanding suburban areas of Dublin, involving the submergence of the existing public vocational schools (the only schools then existing in these areas), in new 'community' schools to be established with the co-operation of religious orders, and in whose management these religious orders would have two-thirds representation. The schools would be vested in trustees to be appointed by the Catholic Archbishop of Dublin (one in the nomination of the Co. Dublin Vocational Education Committee), so that the only publicly-aided education to be provided in these new suburban areas would be in Catholic-owned schools.

But this proposal had to be modified as a result of pressure in the Dail from the opposition Fine Gael and Labour parties. The Minister eventually agreed that he, rather than the Catholic Archbishop of Dublin, would appoint the trustees (although two of these could still be nominated by the religious orders concerned and one by the local Vocational Education

Committee), and that a proposed clause in the trust deed, under which a teaching appointment could be vetoed by the management board on 'faith and morals' grounds, should be dropped. It was also agreed that two of the six board members should be elected by the parents, and two, rather than four, be chosen by the religious orders concerned, although this was not to take effect in the new suburban schools until three years after the establishment. At the time of writing agreement has not yet been reached on the terms of the proposed trust deed, but Protestant educational spokesmen have accepted the general outline of the revised arrangements.

One other significant change in the educational system needs to be mentioned. Whereas in the Republic the Department of Education, inheriting the role of the pre-independence Board of Intermediate Commissioners, remains in full control of the curriculum and post-primary examination system, through which it implements the government's policy of making Irish an essential examination subject in post-primary schools, in Northern Ireland since 1961 there has been a devolution of responsibility for these academic aspects of post-primary education to successive Committees, which after almost a decade of existence as non-statutory bodies were in 1970 replaced by a statutory Northern Ireland Schools Examination Council which conducts examinations through Examination Boards.

There is, accordingly, a considerable contrast to-day between the organisation of education in the North and the Republic, but in neither area has any real progress been made towards breaking down the sectarian barriers in education. The resistance of the Roman Catholic Church to integrated education is unabated, and any suggestion that such integration might assist the problem of inter-communal relations in the North has been rejected, with the argument that separate education is not the *cause* of bigotry in the North—an argument that ignores the possibility that the segregation of Protestants and Catholics at school, while not being the *cause* of communal bitterness, may help to maintain and indeed further the polarisation of the two communities.

Are the differences between the two educational systems, as they have evolved, reconcilable? To this question one must answer that the differences that have grown up between the two systems are not of fundamental significance, as may be seen from the fact that both systems are accepted by the same religious authorities; there could therefore be no fundamental difficulty about creating a single educational system.

At the same time the situation in the Republic reflects a very high degree of commitment by the Catholic Church authorities to the segregated educational system; whatever concessions to change in other sectors the Catholic ecclesiastical authorities in the Republic may have made in recent decades, there is no sign of any willingness to budge on this issue. Indeed the fact that the Fianna Fail Government felt it necessary to shape its 1971 school rationalisation programme initially along lines that involved an actual extension of segregation, suggests a desire on the part of the authorities of the Catholic Church to harden attitudes on this issue.

It must, however, be said that attachment to the system of segregated primary and secondary schools is not confined to the Catholic Hierarchy; it is probable that if the Irish people in the Republic were consulted directly on this issue, there would be a very large majority in favour of maintaining the segregated system, not only amongst Catholics but also amongst many Protestants who fear the effects of the *Ne Temere* decree and subsequent Vatican legislation under which Catholics contracting a mixed marriage are required by their Church to agree, and to secure the agreement of their intended spouse to bring the children of the union up as Catholics.

At the same time the large minority of parents in the Republic whose children attend vocational schools (about a quarter at the time of writing, but this share is growing rapidly, the *increase* in school population being about evenly divided among secondary and vocational schools), are quite content with this system and many would resist any change in it. This may to some degree reflect, however, the fact that in the more conservative rural areas such schools are often *de facto* Catholic schools, so that in practice the issue of inter-denominational education arises only in urban areas and in certain border districts; moreover, in almost all cases where the schools are in fact mixed, the Catholics are in a vast majority.

In Northern Ireland attitudes may be somewhat different, but are hard to assess. There are many on both sides of the religious divide who are conscious of what they feel to be the divisive effects of the segregated educational system. Moreover, because religious differences are so deep, and because the Protestants are either a large minority or else an actual majority of the population, fears of the effects of the *Ne Temere* decree are less acute—although resentment against it may well be stronger. There is also the fact that the Presbyterians, a small minority of the Protestant population in the Republic but providing half of the total number of Protestants in Northern Ireland, have always tended to favour mixed education on principle. Finally, it is noteworthy that in the Rose Survey of Catholic and Protestant attitudes in Northern Ireland in 1968, the principal results of which are summarised in Chapter 5, there was overwhelming Catholic approval for a campaign to mix Catholics and Protestants together in State schools—62% approved, 28% disapproved and 10% had no opinion. We do not, of course, know how attitudes to this issue, as to so much else, may have changed since 1968.

One final point on education in Northern Ireland is, perhaps, worth making. Quite a number of the leaders of the minority to-day were the early beneficiaries of the post-war educational reforms in the North. These reforms opened up post-primary education to children of working-class parents who would not otherwise have had such an opportunity. In the 1960s the beneficiaries of this education amongst the Catholic community began to challenge the hitherto largely rural middle-class leadership of the minority, through such bodies as the Civil Rights Association and, later, the Social Democratic and Labour Party. It will be interesting to see whether the Republic experiences a similar upheaval in its political system in the 1970s and 1980s as a result of the introduction of free post-primary education in 1967, just twenty years after the similar educational revolution in the North.

THE PROTESTANT CHURCHES IN NORTHERN IRELAND

Before turning to the economic field, a comment must be made about the influence of the Protestant Churches in Northern Ireland. It would be quite wrong to ignore the fact that the Protestant Churches have exercised a very considerable political influence in the province—different in style from the kind of influence wielded by the Catholic Church in the Republic, but none the less very significant. Reference has already been made to the influence of the Protestant Churches on educational legislation; they have also had a powerful effect on licensing laws—arguably greater than the influence exerted by the Catholic Church in the Republic on the evolution of these laws; moreover the strongly Sabbatarian tradition of Northern Protestantism has continued to influence the availability of many facilities on Sundays. Even in the late 1960s the issue of the opening of children's playgrounds in public parks on Sundays was a major source of controversy, in which not only Unionists but members of the Northern Ireland Labour Party were to be found resisting a liberalisation of these restrictive provisions. To the average Catholic in the Republic this smacks as much of 'theocracy' as any features of his laws, and he finds it difficult to follow the logic of Northern Protestant reasoning which rejects the influence of Catholic Church teaching on laws in the Republic but seeks to impose Protestant Sabbatarianism of a particularly rigid kind on the Catholic population of the North.

Moreover, the direct involvement of Protestant clergy in politics is a feature of Northern Ireland that has no equivalent in the Republic, where Catholic priests, brothers and nuns are by convention excluded from any participation in party politics. It has been said that few Unionist branches in Northern Ireland are without a clergyman amongst their members; as a practising politician the author has never heard of *any* Catholic clergyman currently engaged in politics at branch level or indeed any other level.

Again, the Orange Order, a specifically religious society, whose raison d'être is the preservation of Protestantism, is directly represented in the Unionist Party to which it elects members in its own right. No political party in the Republic would for a moment tolerate such representation for the nearest equivalents to the Orange Order in that part of Ireland—viz. the Ancient Order of Hibernians or the Knights of St. Columbanus. Moreover, until the latter part of the 1960s membership of the Orange Order was regarded as a prerequisite for membership of the Unionist Parliamentary Party and the Northern Ireland Government, and even to-day only a small minority of Northern Unionist MPs are not members of the Order.

This pattern contrasts markedly with the situation in the Republic where only a small minority of politicians belong to religious organisations of this kind, and where, indeed, such bodies are regarded with considerable suspicion by many politicians. The suggestion that a politician in the Republic might be influenced in his actions by membership of such a body would be very damaging to him in the eyes of his colleagues and of public opinion generally.

Here as elsewhere the two parts of Ireland have followed very different paths since independence. Such limited involvement by Catholic clergy in politics as existed before independence has disappeared completely in the Repbulic, whereas in Northern Ireland the link between Protestant Churches and Unionism has if anything been reinforced over this half-century, and a measure of involvement by Catholic clergy in the politics of the Nationalist Party in Northern Ireland has also survived. Whatever fears Northern Protestants may have about the influence of the Catholic Church on the attitudes of their flock to political issues, or past intervention of the Catholic Hierarchy in legislative matters, are closely paralleled by the incredulity and distaste with which Catholics in the Republic view the involvement of Protestant churchmen in Northern Ireland politics.

FINANCIAL AND ECONOMIC DIFFERENCES

Among the fresh obstacles to a united Ireland that have developed since 1920 are economic and financial ones. The development of the Welfare State has introduced a much larger element of transfer of resources between rich and poor regions than existed fifty years ago. As a result of this Northern Ireland is now heavily subsidised by Great Britain to an extent far beyond anything that existed in 1920. The Republic, on the other hand, benefits from no such subsidies, apart from a link with the UK deficiency payment system in respect of small quantities of beef, mutton and lamb; this concession is worth a couple of million pounds a year at most, and will disappear with EEC membership.

Because the amounts now involved in inter-regional transfers between Great Britain and Northern Ireland are so substantial they pose a serious obstacle to-day to the re-unification of Ireland—and also, it must be said, to any unilateral declaration of independence by Northern Ireland.

An analysis of these subsidies as they stood in 1967/68 is contained in an article by Mr. John Simpson entitled 'Regional Analysis: the Northern Ireland Experience'.[6] His conclusion, set out in the table below, is that in that year Northern Ireland's

[6] *Economic and Social Review*, Vol. 2, No. 4, July, 1971. Certain misprints in the table as published there are corrected in the version published here by courtesy of John Simpson.

TABLE 1.   CENTRAL GOVERNMENT TRANSACTIONS
IN NORTHERN IRELAND   1967/68   (£ m.)

Current Revenue			Current Expenditure		
Reserved Taxes etc.			*By Northern Ireland Ministries*		
Income tax	51		Goods and services	63	
Corporation tax	19	(23)	Subsidies	14	
Customs and excise	99	(85)	Grants to persons	32	
Other	5		Grants to Local		
less Cost of collection	−2		Authorities	44	
Transferred Taxes			Debt interest	14	
S.E.T. (net)	6		*Paid to UK Government*		
Motor vehicles	7		Land annuities, pen-		
Estate duties	2		sions, Imperial		
Excise (mainly betting)	1		Contributions	1	(71)
Stamp duties	1		Agricultural subsidies	—	(25)
Other Revenue			*Surplus on current*		
Interest on advances	13		*transactions*	58	(−63)
Land annuities	1		*Capital transfers*		
Factory rents	2		*(mainly industrial*		
Loan (industrial)			*assistance)*	32	
repayments	1		*Surplus for capital*		
Other	4		*purposes*	26	(−95)
Transfers from UK Government					
Social Service					
agreement	10	(—)			
Agricultural					
remoteness grant	2	(—)			
R.E.P. assistance	4	(—)			
TOTAL	226	(200)	TOTAL	226	(200)

Capital Receipts					
Current surplus	26	(−95)	Government capital		
			formation	27	
Borrowing (net)			Lending (net) to Local		
—from reserves etc.	7		Authorities and public		
—from local sources	5		corporations	37	
—other (mainly UK			Shortfall on attri-		
Government)	26	(37)	bution	—	(110)
	64	(−46)		64	(−46)

NOTE: Figures in brackets are based on estimates if Northern Ireland collected its own taxes at UK rates and had to pay its own attributable costs in the United Kingdom while maintaining current standards of expenditure (excluding National Insurance).

This table is published by courtesy of John Simpson of Queens University, and is reproduced from the July, 1971, issue of the Economic and Social Review, *with some corrections of misprints.*

current revenue was £121 m. below what would have been necessary if the province had had to be self-supporting—levying taxes at UK rates, maintaining current British standards of expenditure, and paying its attributable cost of UK overheads such as defence and the monarchy. A further shortfall of £16 m. existed with respect to the National Insurance Fund, which was met by a re-insurance provision involving a further subsidy of this amount from Britain. On the other hand he estimates that if Northern Ireland had not been part of the United Kingdom, its government could have borrowed £11 m. more to meet capital investment needs. The net deficiency in that year, therefore, as estimated by John Simpson, would have been £126 m.

These transfers have, however, increased very substantially since 1967/68. The table below sets out estimated inter-regional current transfer figures for 1971/72, comparing them with the 1967/68 figures in the table (the details of these 1971/72 calculations are to be found in Appendix I):

INTER-REGIONAL TRANSFERS FROM GREAT BRITAIN TO NORTHERN IRELAND

	1967/68	1971/72
Under-attribution of Corporation Tax	−4	−2
Over-attribution of Customs & Excise	14	37
Social Services Agreement Transfers	10	57
Agricultural Remoteness Grant	2	2
Regional Employment Premium Assistance	4	11
Agricultural Subsidies	25	30
TOTAL—DIRECT TRANSFERS	51	135
Imperial Contribution Shortfall	70	85
TOTAL	121	220

This calculation must, however, be qualified in several respects. First of all, while it indicates the scale of direct subsidisation it also includes an estimate of indirect subsidies as a result of Northern Ireland not being called upon to pay more than a nominal contribution of £1 m. towards the UK 'overheads' which consist very largely of defence. It does not follow that Northern Ireland within a peaceful united Ireland would have to pay an equivalent sum. Thus the Republic's defence bill in 1971/72 was £22½ m., and on a pro-rata basis that of

Northern Ireland would be only £11 m. (In a UDI situation, however, the cost of Northern Ireland internal security and defence might be much nearer the figure derived by pro-rating British defence expenditure; the forces engaged in Northern Ireland after internment in August, 1971, were about twice as numerous as the Irish Army, and better-equipped and paid, and it seems improbable that a UDI Northern Ireland would have a less serious security problem than that which existed at that period.)

On the other hand, the figure of £220 m. given above for 1971/72 does not include the re-insurance provisions covering the National Insurance Fund, under which a further direct subsidy of £15 m. in 1971/72 was payable.

Allowing for these two factors (and it must be said that the assumption that Northern Ireland defence and internal security would cost only £11 m. a year in a united Ireland may be very optimistic), the preservation of existing standards in Northern Ireland without additional taxation there, would have cost about £160–170 m. in 1971/72 had Northern Ireland been part of a united Ireland in that year.

The raising of the Republic's health service and social service provisions to the Northern level of eligibility and benefit would have cost it a further £150 m. in 1969/70, the latest year for which such a calculation can be made (see Appendix II for details). The raising to the Northern Ireland level of the Republic's provision for education and public capital investment, including housing, would have involved very considerable additional sums on top of this.

These figures should be seen against the background of a 1971/72 current revenue position of about £385 m. in Northern Ireland and £570 m. in the Republic.

The implications of these figures for re-unification are considered in Chapter 10.

PARTITION AS A BREAK ON NORTH-SOUTH DIVERGENCES

Having laid such emphasis upon the way in which Partition has itself aggravated differences between the North and the Republic, and has created fresh differences where none previously existed, it must in fairness be added that in the Republic conscious efforts have been made to retain some former links, and to prevent the emergence of gaps or differences in particular areas of economic and social life.

Most of the all-Ireland vocational bodies that existed in 1920 have been maintained, even though this has in some instances involved the Republic in an exercise in self-restraint. Thus the Irish Congress of Trade Unions, although it has gone through some changes and some vicissitudes in the past fifty years, remains an all-Ireland organisation. This has involved a delicate balancing act with respect to English-based and Irish-based unions; for a period in the 1940s and 1950s this balance was lost, and two trade union congresses co-existed unhappily, but in 1959 unity was restored. This trade union unity has been an important, although unfortunately not a decisive factor, in community relations in Northern Ireland, where the fact that workers from both the majority and the minority are members of the same trade union movement has helped at certain periods to prevent an escalation of inter-community bitterness. Many, although not all, sporting organisations have also continued to be organised on an all-Ireland basis. This is true, for example, not alone of the Gaelic Athletic Association, but also of the Irish Rugby Football Union[7] but association football is 'partitioned'. The Churches, of course, have maintained their all-Ireland character, Armagh in Northern Ireland is for both the Roman Catholic Church and the (Anglican) Church of Ireland, the see of the Primate of All Ireland, and the Presbyterian and Methodist Churches are also organised on an all-Ireland basis. Many other vocational bodies, including professional bodies, have, however, become 'partitioned', or, if established since 1920, have been established separately in Northern Ireland and the Republic.

An important effect of the division of Ireland has been the extent to which in matters such as banking, currency and standard time, the Republic has felt obliged to keep step with the United Kingdom, in order to avoid creating fresh divergences between North and South; it is almost as if governments in the Republic felt it necessary to compensate for the cultural divisions created since 1920. At times this policy of keeping in step has had its ludicrous sides. Thus in 1968 the Republic precipitately followed the United Kingdom in extending

[7] While the all-Ireland character of these bodies is of considerable significance unfortunately within Northern Ireland they are polarised on a religious basis—almost all Roman Catholic children being brought up to play Gaelic games while in Protestant schools Rugby football is played. In the Republic the division is more on a class than a religious basis.

'Summer Time' to the whole year—and in 1971, equally pre-cipitately, it reversed engines and followed Britain in reverting to standard time in Winter. This exercise was all the more remarkable in view of the fact that up to 1916, as an integral part of the United Kingdom, Ireland had its own time, twenty-five minutes in advance of GMT! The sensitivity of an inde-pendent Irish Government to time differences between the Republic and the United Kingdom would seem to have arisen from a concern to maintain the same time on both sides of the Irish border.

Again, when the United Kingdom decimalised its currency in February, 1971, the Irish Government followed suit, and despite the strong arguments in favour of a different system of decimalisation, adopted the British 'heavy pound' system—viz. retaining the pound sterling and dividing it into one hundred 'new penny' units. A 'two shilling' pound, decimalised to pro-vide units of about the same magnitude as in most Continental countries, was advocated by the Federation of Irish Industries, among others, but this, and the other alternative of a 'pound-mil' system, was rejected by the Government, which in this connection also appears to have been largely influenced by a desire to maintain the same system of currency on both sides of the Border.

This close alignment of Irish policies in such matters with the policies adopted by the United Kingdom Government has had a counterpart in foreign policy. Superficially the foreign policy of the Republic may appear to have diverged notably from that of the United Kingdom; Ireland remained neutral in the Second World War, refused to join NATO in 1949, and has tended to align itself with anti-colonial sentiment at the United Nations. What is surprising, however, is not that such diver-gences have existed, but that they have been relatively speaking so limited, given the very clear divergence of interest between a small country with a large agricultural sector and its very much larger and highly-industrialised neighbour.

Leaving the Northern Ireland problem on one side, the ex-treme economic dependence of Ireland on the United Kingdom has been the greatest single problem facing the Republic in the external field, especially in view of Britain's traditional 'cheap food' policy, and that country's ability, since the introduction of the deficiency payment system after the Second World War, to operate this policy without too many inhibitions concerning its impact on its own farmers. Logically the Republic should in its own economic interest have sought to minimise this dependence and have established close economic links with other countries; a policy for which the establishment of the European Economic Community, and the development of its common agricultural policy, provided fresh opportunities. Instead Irish Governments have tended to intensify rather than to weaken their trade links with the United Kingdom, e.g. the Anglo-Irish Free Trade Area Agreement of 1965, and such a policy is difficult to explain except in terms of a concern to maintain close links with a United Kingdom which still incorporated a part of Ireland. Were it not for this consideration one might have expected the Irish Government to have pursued more actively the possibilities of a link with the EEC even during the period when the negotiations for UK membership were in abeyance.

It would perhaps be a mistake to make too much of the inhibiting effect of Partition upon the development of an independent Irish foreign policy, but it would equally be an error to dismiss this factor as irrelevant; it has almost certainly played some part in the close alignment of Ireland with a Britain whose interests have diverged so notably from those of its smaller neighbour.

PARTITION INHIBITING DEVELOPMENT OF IDEOLOGICAL POLITICS

There is another way in which the division of Ireland affected both parts of the country in a similar sense: because of Partition, politics both North and South have tended to remain frozen in a pre-ideological state. This is most obvious, of course, in Northern Ireland, where the Protestant and Catholic working-classes continued after 1920 to support extremely conservative parties lacking in any political programme intended to or likely to serve the interests of these workers. But Partition has also had somewhat similar effects in the Republic, where the astute playing of the 'anti-partition' card, especially at election times, has contributed to the ability of the latterly very conservative Fianna Fail party to remain in power throughout 85% of the forty years from 1932 to 1972.

Fianna Fail's support amongst workers has been influenced by other factors also—e.g. the industrial employment created by its protection policy in the 1930s and 1940s, and the mere fact that it was in office for most of a period during which the gradual growth of prosperity and changing social attitudes in the world contributed to various not very radical social reforms in Ireland. But by successfully identifying itself with Irish nationalism, and by taking the lead in propaganda campaigns against Partition—campaigns destined for domestic consumption and sterilely counter-productive in terms of their impact on the North—Fianna Fail consolidated the support of social groups whose economic interests were not adequately served by the party's policies, and helped to prevent an ideological orientation of Irish politics on a left/right basis. The small Irish Labour Party never succeeded in making much progress in the face of this situation—it has never won more than 15% of the seats in the Dail—and only a leftward shift in the principal opposition party, Fine Gael, in and after 1964, has so far offered any prospect of creating a more normal and constructive party alignment in the Republic.

In Northern Ireland the emergence of the Social Democratic and Labour Party provides an indication of a similar belated trend towards a more left/right orientation in politics, but its identification with the minority, the fact that this party and the Northern Ireland Labour Party have not formed a common front, and the polarisation of the Protestant and Catholic working classes has more than offset any progress towards a more normal political alignment in the North.

It is idle to speculate as to what political alignments might have emerged in Ireland had its unity been maintained fifty years ago, but at the very least there would have been a much better chance of a more rational division in Irish political life, and a strong possibility that Catholic and Protestant workers North and South, might have united in defence of their common interests.

The division of Ireland has thus had very considerable effects upon the development of the island in the past half century. Although the Republic has gone to some trouble to prevent divisions emerging between North and South in such relatively unimportant matters as currency and time, in other respects the two areas have grown much further apart, culturally and economically, while at the same time a natural political evolution has been stunted by the continued and even aggravated polarisation of the two communities in Northern Ireland and the employment of the partition issue for political purposes in the Republic. These effects were undoubtedly under-estimated, in so far as they were foreseen at all, in 1920–1922. The self-perpetuating nature of a division of this kind within a hitherto united country is something that one learns only from bitter experience.

4. Economic Differences

HAVING considered the historical development of this problem, the reasons why Ireland came to be politically divided fifty years ago, and the impact of this division upon the two parts of the country since then, it is time to look at the situation as it now exists in the two parts of Ireland. How fundamental are the differences that divide these two areas to-day, whether they ante-date the settlement of 1920–1922 or have arisen out of the political division then effected? And are these differences such as to preclude any possible reunion of the two areas within a shared political framework? Or are they rather the kind of differences which exist within many federal States, or even within some unitary ones?

One must, of course, distinguish between inter-community differences within Northern Ireland and differences which separate the two parts of Ireland. The former are largely, although not exclusively, psychological; the latter are in many respects much more concrete. Which of them—the psychological or the concrete differences—are likely to prove the more intractable is a nice question.

Northern Ireland as it has evolved under fifty years of Home Rule is to-day marked by a curious amalgam of pre-Home Rule Irish features, British elements, and local post-1920 innovations —some designed to consolidate the power of the majority, but others representing the normal evolution of a State in the mid-twentieth century. The whole society is, however, dominated by the inter-community divisions, which even before the recent troubles, affected—infected, one might rather say— every aspect of life in the area. In many respects Northern Ireland is in advance of the Republic; its social services are much more wide-ranging and, as has already been said, the benefits paid are much more generous than across the Border; its agriculture, aided by UK deficiency payments, is much more prosperous; its new industries include plants far larger than any yet in production in the Republic; its industrial training provisions are more extensive and enlightened; its physical planning arrangements are arguably more impressive.

Yet all that this might in other circumstances imply is vitiated by the psychological gulf within this society and by the self-perpetuating mutual fear which has corroded relations between the majority and the minority there. By contrast the Republic, which has less to offer under all these headings, where living standards are on average somewhat lower than in Northern Ireland, and where many social problems are more acute, is a normal society in which people have lived together in reasonable harmony and without fear.

In contrasting the two parts of Ireland in economic or social terms, this difference must never be forgotten. It would be all too easy to draw up an economic and social balance-sheet showing the North to have distinctly more assets than the Republic, but the fact remains that remarkably few people in the Republic would seek to enjoy the benefits of life in community-divided Northern Ireland were they given an opportunity of doing so. Indeed, even before the disturbances began in 1969 there were very few people in the Republic who even considered visiting Northern Ireland—in contrast to the quite large flow of visitors in the other direction.

A. POPULATION, EMPLOYMENT, EMIGRATION

Comparisons between the two areas are facilitated by the fact that the population ratio is almost precisely two-to-one, in the Republic's favour. Of Ireland's estimated 4,499,000 inhabitants in 1971, 1,528,000 lived in the North, and 2,971,000 in the Republic. One hundred and thirty years ago, just before the Great Famine, the population ratio was quite different: then the area now comprised in the Republic had four times the population of the territory of Northern Ireland. In the fifty years after the Famine the population of what is now the Republic halved, whereas that of the six north-eastern counties dropped by only a quarter. In the first sixty years of this century the population decline in the Republic continued, but that of Northern Ireland rose slowly but steadily. Because the population decline in the north-east was both slower and of briefer duration, and because the population of this area has been recovering throughout this century, it stands to-day at a level little below its 1841 figure, whereas that of the Republic is well below half the level of 130 years ago.

During the 1960s the population of the Republic started to rise again. Because of a less favourable age-structure (itself a consequence of high levels of emigration in the past), the birth-rate in the Republic has been fractionally lower than that in Northern Ireland despite a somewhat higher fertility rate, and, largely for the same reason, the death rate has been somewhat higher. The natural increase in population—excess of births over deaths—has thus been somewhat less in the Republic, so that if no one emigrated or immigrated the population would have risen by about 1% a year during this decade, as compared with 1.15% per annum in Northern Ireland.

But the Republic has traditionally suffered from a higher rate of emigration than Northern Ireland. This has partly been because of a less favourable employment situation but has also been due to the fact that more generous unemployment payments in Northern Ireland have tended to encourage those who cannot secure employment to remain there, whereas in the Republic the lower level of unemployment payments, and the contrast between these sums and what have been available in Britain, have encouraged the unemployed of the Republic to emigrate rather than to remain on the unemployment register at home.

Since the early 1960s, however, the relationship between the net emigration rates in the two areas has been more or less reversed, the Northern Ireland annual rate remaining constant at .47% to .48% a year, while that in the Republic has fallen from .56% to .42%. As a result and despite the higher rate of natural increase in the North, the rate of population growth in Northern Ireland was not significantly higher than in the Republic.[1]

The rate of emigration is, of course, primarily a function of employment opportunities. This does not, of course mean that

[1] These figures are based on the provisional Census of Population returns for 1971. In Northern Ireland there was political opposition to the taking of Census in certain areas, which could have contributed to under-recording of the population, and thus over-estimation of net emigration, but it seems unlikely that the scale of under-recording could have been sufficient to affect the basic validity of the picture indicated above.

all those who emigrate are looking for jobs—some are the
dependants of job-seeking emigrants, and especially when
during a recession people with family commitments lose their
jobs and emigrate, the ratio of dependants to job-seeking emigrants can rise sharply. Moreover, it may well be true that even
if employment opportunities existed in Ireland for all those
entering the labour market, some would still choose to emigrate
either because of family links with earlier emigrants, or because
of a preference for the very different environment of Britain or
the United States. (In its Report on Full Employment in 1967[2]
the National Industrial Economic Council assumed that voluntary emigration of this kind from the Republic was of the order
of 5,000 a year—rather less than 10% of the numbers reaching
maturity in Ireland annually—but they pointed out that this
could be little more than a guess and suggested that a study of
the factors influencing the decision to emigrate or to stay in
Ireland would constitute a fruitful field for research by the
Economic and Social Research Institute.)

Nevertheless the fundamental cause of *most* emigration is the
absence of employment opportunities in Ireland for those leaving school or university or leaving sectors of the economy such
as agriculture or declining industries such as linen in Northern
Ireland. North and South differ markedly in the pattern of
their employment, but both suffer from the existence of large
sectors within which employment has been declining for decades.
In view of the fact that in 1951 no less than 40% of all jobs in
Northern Ireland, and 44% of those in the Republic, were in
such sectors of declining employment, it is scarcely surprising
that in the 1950s and 1960s no significant increase in total employment was achieved; in the Republic, indeed, in the 1950s,
total employment declined quite sharply.

The arithmetic of this is quite simple. In a country whose
economy has no significant sectors of declining employment a
natural increase in population of 1% a year can be absorbed
by an equivalent annual increase in total employment. But if
40% of jobs are in sectors within which employment is declining
at 3% a year—as was approximately the case in both parts of
Ireland in the 1950s—then in order to secure an increase of 1%
a year in *total* employment, the healthy 60% of the economy
would need to expand its employment by almost 4% annually,

[2] Report on Full Employment, No. 18, National Industrial Council,
March, 1967, Pr. 9188, pp. 23–24.

TABLE 2. POPULATION AND EMIGRATION

A. POPULATION (in thousands)

	1841	1901	1951	1961	1966*	1971	Average Annual Percentage Change		
							1951-61	1961-66	1966-71
Republic of Ireland	6,529	3,222	2,961	2,818	2,884*	2,971	−.49%	+.46%	+.60%
Northern Ireland	1,649	1,237	1,371	1,425	1,479*	1,528	+.39%	+.75%*	+.65%*
IRELAND	8,178	4,459	4,332	4,243	4,363	4,499	−.21%	+.56%	+.62%

B. NATURAL INCREASE AND NET EMIGRATION, 1961–1971 (in thousands)

	Republic of Ireland				Northern Ireland				Ireland			
	Number		Rate per 1,000		Number		Rate per 1,000		Number		Rate per 1,000	
	1961–66	1966–71	1961–66	1966–71	1961–66*	1966–71*	1961–66*	1966–71*	1961–66	1966–71	1961–66	1966–71
Births	313	314	21.9	21.5	166	164	22.9	21.8	479	478	22.3	21.6
Less Deaths	−166	−165	−11.65	−11.25	−79	−79	−10.8	−10.5	−246	−244	−11.4	−11.0
Natural Increase	146	149	10.25	10.25	88	85	12.1	11.3	234	234	10.9	10.6
Net Emigration	−81	−62	−5.65	−4.25	−34	−36	−4.7	−4.8	−115	−98	−5.3	−4.4
POPULATION CHANGE	+66	+87	+4.6	+6.0	+54	+49	+7.5	+6.5	+120	+136	+5.6	+6.2

* The 1966 Census in Northern Ireland was taken in October instead of in April and the Northern Ireland population figures for 1966 in this table are estimated April figures.

to cater for those leaving the declining sectors as well as for the natural increase in the labour force.

Such a rate of increase in employment outside the declining sectors implies a remarkably high rate of expansion of output in these sectors—for labour productivity, or output per worker, increases over time, and rises fastest where output itself is expanding rapidly. Growth rates of 8% or 9% could thus be needed outside the declining sectors if in the expanding sectors employment were to increase by the required 4% a year. Such a rate of economic growth would be quite exceptional, and nothing like it was in fact achieved in Ireland North or South in the 1950s.

At the same time the problem posed by these declining sectors is a self-resolving one in the long run. By 1961 the proportion of employment in these declining activities had been reduced from 40% to 30% in Northern Ireland, and by 1971 it was down to 18%. In the Republic progress was less rapid; whereas in Northern Ireland the problem of declining employment has been to a large degree an industrial one—over half of the decline in employment having occurred in the industrial sector (shipbuilding, linen and cotton, and clothing)—in the Republic virtually the whole problem has been in the agricultural sector, for shipbuilding and linen and cotton in the Republic are small industries in which in fact employment rose slightly during these decades. Partly for this reason but mainly because even outside these sectors employment in the Republic declined in the 1950s, the share of employment in agriculture, clothing, linen and cotton and shipbuilding, fell less sharply in the Republic than in Northern Ireland between 1951 and 1961 from 44% to 39%, but in 1971 it had been reduced to about 29%.

The diminishing scale of the problem of declining employment sectors was reflected in a reversal of the downward trend of total employment during the 1960s. Increases in employment in expanding sectors outweighed the erosion of jobs in the declining sectors between 1961 and 1966. In the latter part of the 1960s, however, the momentum of industrial expansion was slowed in both areas, yielding an expansion in employment which in Northern Ireland was actually insufficient to offset the decrease in employment in the declining employment sectors; as a result total employment declined slightly in Northern Ireland and it remained static in the Republic between 1966 and 1971.

TABLE 3. EMPLOYMENT CHANGES, 1951–1971

Sector	Republic of Ireland				Northern Ireland				Ireland			
	1951	1961	1966	1971*	1951	1961	1966	1971*	1951	1961	1966	1971
Agriculture	490	371	326	274	98	71	53	43	588	442	379	317
Linen & Cotton	4	5	6	6	65	42	31	23	69	47	37	29
Clothing & Footwear	36	29	28	31	31	25	24	25	67	54	52	56
Shipbuilding	1	1	1	1	23	22	13	10	24	23	14	12
DECLINING SECTORS	531	406	361	313	217	160	121	101	748	566	482	414
Other Manufacturers	143	143	163	185	75	89	112	117	218	232	275	302
Construction	85	60	74	79	40	42	54	53	125	102	128	132
Other Sectors	458	444	468	491	214	248	276	280	672	692	744	771
EXPANDING SECTORS	686	647	705	755	329	379	442	450	1,015	1,026	1,147	1,205
TOTAL EMPLOY-MENT	1,217	1,053	1,066	1,068	546	539	563	551	1,763	1,592	1,629	1,619

* Estimated.

The problem of the sectors of declining employment is now somewhat less acute in Northern Ireland than in the Republic. Quite apart from the fact that these sectors to-day comprise only 18% of the North's total employment, as against 29% in the Republic, there is perhaps a greater prospect of reasonable stability in employment in some of these sectors in Northern Ireland. It is true that the 18,000 jobs in shipbuilding and air-craft construction remain vulnerable, but the linen and cotton industry, although unlikely to be buoyant, may not experience a continued erosion of employment in the years ahead on the scale suffered in the 1950s and 1960s, and the clothing industry was already showing signs of some buoyancy in employment as well as output in the second half of the 1960s. Moreover, agriculture in Northern Ireland now has such a small labour force that while further reductions in employment in this sector are inevitable, they are unlikely in absolute terms to be on such a significant scale in future.

In the Republic by contrast, the agricultural sector is bound to experience a continuous decline in employment for many years to come, on a scale that will certainly be significant in terms of the number of new jobs required in other sectors to offset these losses.[3] Nevertheless even in the Republic the decline in agricultural employment measured in absolute terms will tend to diminish in the years ahead as the agricultural labour force experiencing this erosion itself declines in absolute terms.

B. INDUSTRY

The structure of industry in Northern Ireland is very different from that of industry in the Republic. In Northern Ireland two sectors of industry are dominant—linen and synthetic textiles, and mechanical engineering, including shipbuilding and air-craft construction. Between them these two sectors account for over 40% of net output of manufacturing industry in Northern

---

[3] In an article in the *Irish Times* (July 14, 1971), reviewing a paper by Dr. Brendan Walsh, the author showed that if there were no further decline in the number of entrants to agriculture, and if the outflow from agriculture was reduced to perhaps 400–500 a year from each age cohort for about five years when those concerned are in their early twenties, the total number of people engaged in agriculture would fall by almost 100,000 in the twenty-five years from 1971 to 1996 simply because of the unbalanced age structure of the agricultural population, with twice as many farmers aged 50–54 as aged 20–24, for example.

Ireland and almost 45% of manufacturing employment. By contrast, despite the existence of a highly protected motor vehicle assembly industry in the Republic, these two sectors account for barely 10% of the net output of manufacturing there, and 12½% of employment.

The industries which exist on a significantly larger scale in the Republic than in Northern Ireland are the processing of livestock products (meat slaughtering and dairying), the woollen and hosiery sections of the textile industry, the paper and printing industries, the chemical and fertiliser industries, building materials, and metals, as well as the 'miscellaneous industries' group, into which fall many of the new industries that have been established in Ireland in the last two decades as a result of the industrial promotion policies of the governments, North and South. These industries account for over half of manufacturing output in the Republic, but for only one-fifth of that of Northern Ireland.

The remaining industries, which are more or less equally represented in both parts of the country, include two of special importance—the food and drink industries (other than the processing of livestock products, which was mentioned above), and clothing. Shirt-making looms larger in Northern Ireland, however, and the manufacture of outerwear is relatively more important in the Republic.

These different industrial patterns reflect in part the traditional concentration of the linen industry and shipbuilding and engineering in Northern Ireland, and of the processing of livestock products in the Republic; in part, the diversifying impact of industrial protection in the Republic; and in part, the effects, of the promotional drive of the past twenty years, which has led to the establishment of an important synthetic textiles complex in Northern Ireland, and of a fairly wide range of new export industries in the Republic.

In many instances there is little to choose between industries North and South of the Border, so far as capital intensity and efficiency are concerned, measuring these in terms of net output per employee. Net output per worker is much higher in Northern Ireland, however, in the case of a miscellaneous group of food and drink industries, for which no breakdown is available, for grain-milling and animal feeding stuffs, for the section of the textile industry which includes the manufacture of synthetics, and for chemicals. On the other hand net output per worker is significantly higher in the building materials and electrical engineering sectors in the Republic. Net output per head for the whole of manufacturing industry is only fractionally higher in Northern Ireland than in the Republic.

One further point of contrast between industry in the two parts of Ireland may be worth making. In 1920 such industry as existed in Ireland was largely Irish-owned and managed; much the greater part of it, of course, was in Northern Ireland. Little was done to safeguard or strengthen indigenous industry in the North, however, with the result that much of it is now in British ownership and many firms have British managers. Even the control of distribution in the main centres in Northern Ireland is now largely in British ownership and under British management. This, together with the influx of new industries into Northern Ireland in the 1950s and 1960s, has radically altered the character of industry in the province; the old idea of self-reliant self-made Northern Irish businessmen as the backbone of the province is now largely a myth. Northern self-reliance has been undermined during fifty years of home rule within the United Kingdom.

By contrast in the Republic the introduction of protection led to the emergence of a large sector of Irish-owned and Irish-managed firms, and most of the distribution sector has also remained in Irish hands, and under Irish management. It is now in the Republic rather than in Northern Ireland that the self-reliant, self-made businessman is now to be found, and professional Irish management is centred in Dublin rather than in Belfast. Neither North nor South of the border has this transformation been fully recognised—the Northerners still cherish their myth, and are largely ignorant of the way in which industry and commerce has developed in the Republic in the past forty years, while in the South the tendency towards a national inferiority complex displays itself not only in relation to Britain but also in relation to Northern Ireland; many people in the Republic are unaware of the extent to which indigenous business, owned and managed by Irish people, is a feature to-day of the Republic rather than Northern Ireland. This has not been radically altered even by the inflow of new foreign industry into the Republic during the 1960s—on the whole this has taken the form of new enterprises rather than take-overs by British firms of established Irish concerns.

TABLE 4. MANUFACTURING INDUSTRY, 1967

Sector	Net Output (£ m.)		Employment (Thousands)		Net Output Per Employee (£)	
	Rep.	N. Ireland	Rep.	N. Ireland	Rep.	N. Ireland
Livestock Products	23.8	11.4	14.2	6.5	1,680	1,760
Grain-Milling & Animal Feeding Stuffs	7.8	8.4	4.7	3.4	1,650	2,490
Other Food & Drink	66.2	47.5	31.5	16.3	1,780	2,920
Linen & Cotton	3.9	28.6	3.7	27.0	1,070	1,060
Wool & Hosiery	17.9	8.8	14.7	7.8	1,220	1,140
Other Textiles	5.6	28.1	4.6	7.6	1,230	3,690
Clothing	17.7	15.9	22.3	22.0	800	730
Timber & Furniture	8.1	4.5	7.7	3.3	1,050	1,390
Paper & Printing	21.5	8.2	15.1	5.4	1,420	1,520
Chemicals	20.2	10.7	7.0	2.2	2,900	4,860
Building Materials	10.6	6.9	4.9	4.2	2,140	1,630
Metals	15.4	1.3	10.4	0.6	1,490	2,100
Electrical Engineering	13.4	13.8	8.5	12.1	1,590	1,150
Mechanical Engineering	3.6	23.9	2.5	15.7	1,480	1,530
Other Engineering & Vehicles	15.1	23.0	11.7	20.0	1,290	1,100
Miscellaneous Industries	25.1	8.2	13.9	4.9	1,800	1,680
	266.0	249.3	177.3	159.8	1,500	1,560

NOTE: These figures are derived from the Censuses of Industrial Production for the Republic and Northern Ireland in 1967. Net output in Northern Ireland has been adjusted to bring it into line with the definition used in the Republic. It should be noted that the Census of Industrial Production is not completely comprehensive; smaller firms are omitted from its coverage.

C. AGRICULTURE

There are similar important differences between agriculture in Northern Ireland and in the Republic. In Northern Ireland over 40% of gross output of agriculture adjusted for inputs of livestock is accounted for by pigs and eggs, whereas in the Republic these intensive products accounted for only 15% of output. A further 40% of Northern Ireland farm output is accounted for by cattle and milk. Cereals play very little part in farm output in Northern Ireland—no wheat is grown and barley and oats represent between them less than 1% of agricultural output. In the Republic on the other hand cattle and milk are more dominant elements in agriculture, accounting for over 55% of output. Eggs, produced for home consumption only, are relatively unimportant, while on the other hand cereals account for 9% of gross output.

The extent to which agriculture in Northern Ireland is more intensive than in the Republic is illustrated by the very much higher rate of inputs of feeding stuffs, fertilisers, etc. whose value is over half that of gross output adjusted for inputs of livestock. In the Republic on the other hand these inputs of feeding stuffs, fertilisers, etc. amounted to only 23% of gross output. Because feed prices in the EEC are higher than in the UK and Ireland, this dependence on inputs of feeding stuffs makes Northern Ireland agriculture rather vulnerable under EEC conditions. Its dependence on imports of store cattle from the Republic may also create problems under EEC conditions, as the Republic may find it more economic within the EEC to divert these store animals into its meat factories, although this is not certain. The North could thus find itself doubly squeezed —with its intensive pig and egg trades hit by higher feed prices, and its cattle trade affected adversely by a reduced flow of store animals from the Republic. By contrast EEC membership will be of very great benefit to agriculture in the Republic, whose principal products—beef, mutton and milk—will benefit from substantial price increases and from securing guaranteed access to an enormous market.

D. Trade

Although the patterns of production, both industrial and agricultural, of the two parts of Ireland are rather divergent, this does not mean that the two economies are to a significant degree inter-dependent, save in so far as there is a flow of livestock between the two areas, dictated in part at least by the operation of the UK deficiency payment scheme for farm products. Each part of the country is in large measure self-sufficient in food production, although the North, does import part of its butter requirements from the Republic, as well as a small part of its sugar requirements. (The Republic is self-sufficient in sugar production, whereas Northern Ireland has no beet sugar plants.)

So far as other products are concerned, there is a limited two-way trade in such products as crude materials (e.g. hides and skins), pharmaceuticals, alcoholic beverages, animal feeding stuffs and building materials, while the North derives about one-eighth of its imports of clothing and footwear from the Republic, and sends about one-fifth of its rather limited exports of iron and steel and metal products to the Republic.

In all, the North obtains about 7% of its imports from the Republic, to which it ships about 4% of its exports. Looked at from the viewpoint of the Republic, the North supplies about 4% of its imports, and takes about 12% of its exports.

In so far as Northern Ireland exports to the Republic are concerned, their small scale may in part reflect the continued existence of tariff restrictions in the Republic, most of which—other than tariffs on foodstuffs—are, however, in process of being removed under the terms of the 1965 Anglo-Irish Free Trade Area Agreement. But it also reflects the highly specialised character of much of Northern Ireland industry which is orientated towards world markets rather than to supplying the relatively limited needs of the rest of Ireland.

The failure of the Republic to export to Northern Ireland a larger share of its diversified industrial production is less easy to explain. Something of a paper curtain seems to have cut off the North from the Republic so far as many manufacturers in the South are concerned; for many of them—e.g. manufacturers in Dublin—markets in Northern Ireland are geographically more accessible than markets in the South and West of the Republic, yet this geographical accessibility does not appear to be reflected in the trade figures, although no tariff or quota restrictions have at any stage impeded such exports, save in the case of goods containing synthetic fibres, which until 1966 were dutiable on importation into Northern Ireland from the Republic. One factor influencing this limited export of manufacturers from the Republic to the North may well be a prejudice in Northern Ireland against goods made in the Republic; there is much incidental evidence of this, but it can scarcely explain fully the remarkably low volume of the Republic's industrial output that is directed towards Northern Ireland—no more than 3% in most industrial groups, rising to about 5% in the case of the building materials sector.

It is clear in any event that the agricultural and industrial economies of the Republic and Northern Ireland despite their rather different structures, are competitive rather than complementary. Even though they have developed rather differently than they might have done had Ireland not been divided fifty years ago, it does not seem probable that the reunification of the country would have any very significant economic effect as a result of opening up new possibilities of internal trade, and in so far as there are potential opportunities for such trade, of a limited character, they will in any event become available through the operation of the Anglo-Irish Free Trade Area Agreement and by the participation of both countries in the European Economic Community: political reunion could add little or nothing by way of closer economic integration than will have been achieved as a result of these developments.

Nor are the effects of the political division significant in economic spheres other than those of agriculture and industry. Thus it proved possible, in the 1960s, despite the political differences between North and South, to organise close co-operation in tourist promotion between the two parts of Ireland, 'selling' Ireland as a unit. This has, indeed, been done to such effect that after the troubles in Northern Ireland began in 1969, tourism in the Republic seems to have suffered from the consequent blurring of distinctions between the two parts of Ireland in the minds of tourists.

E. Industrial Development

In both parts of Ireland the 1950s and 1960s saw the emergence of positive campaigns to encourage industrial development. In the Republic this involved the reversal of the xenophobic industrial policy launched in 1932 when the introduction of large-scale industrial protection was accompanied by legislation designed to prevent foreign interests from having majority control over manufacturing companies. This legislation against foreign involvement in Irish industry was prompted by a desire to ensure that the new industrial development created by tariff and quota protection would be Irish in ownership and control. Nevertheless, in conjunction with an emphasis on import-replacement in the home market, which played down the importance of industrial exports, this policy had the effect of discouraging external investment even in new export-orientated industries.

By the end of the 1940s the full benefits of industrial protection had been secured; almost everything that could be manufactured in the Republic with the benefit of protection was by then being produced, and it became desirable to re-orientate . Irish industrial policy towards exports—encouraging the newly-established protected industries to look to export markets for growth, and seeking to attract new foreign-owned firms to Ireland to participate in this expansion of Irish industrial exports. The first step in this direction was taken in 1949, with the establishment of the Industrial Development Authority; other significant steps were the introduction in 1952 of industrial grants to encourage new industrial development in the less developed regions of the north and west; the extension of these grants to the rest of the country in 1956; the introduction of export tax reliefs also in the same year; and finally the announcement in 1958 of the intention to remove the restrictions on external ownership of Irish industry—a decision that was implemented gradually during the following ten years.

Meanwhile in Northern Ireland the promotion of industrial development was also undertaken from the late 1940s onwards. Until the mid-1960s the Northern Ireland industrial promotion programme, which employed generous industrial grants but did not offer tax reliefs, tended to concentrate on the attraction of British and American firms. It was only in the latter part of the 1960s that Northern Ireland joined the Republic in actively seeking to interest Continental firms in locating factories in Ireland.

A feature of the Northern Ireland industrial development programme was its success in attracting relatively large firms to Northern Ireland, especially in the 1950s and early 1960s. In particular the Northern Ireland Government succeeded in attracting to its territory a number of major synthetic textile plants, as a result of which the province became a centre for the manufacture of synthetics within the United Kingdom, thus helping to replace the declining traditional textile industries of Northern Ireland. Between 1961 and 1967 the value of net output of 'miscellaneous textiles'—the category that includes synthetics—increased almost sevenfold, from £4 m. to £27 m., expanding its share of total Northern Ireland textiles output from 14% to 47%.

In the Republic the new industries attracted during the 1960s were more diverse, both in their national origins (roughly one-quarter coming from Britain, one-quarter from the United States, one-quarter from Germany and one-quarter from other countries) and in their range of products; they also tended to be smaller, few of the male-employing industries having more than 300–400 workers. In contrast to what happened in the case of tourism, the industrial promotion programmes of the two parts of Ireland were never co-ordinated; they remained competitive throughout the whole period.

Associated with industrial development was the emergence of physical planning in both parts of Ireland. In Northern Ireland planning tended to concentrate development in a relatively few areas, outside Belfast but, until 1968 at least, within the Belfast region. The aim was to create alternative growth centres to Belfast, but within the prosperous eastern part of the province—a policy naturally bitterly resisted by the less developed western part of Northern Ireland, whose capital, Derry, was neglected throughout most of this period. Only in 1968 shortly before the Civil Rights movement was launched, was a positive effort made to secure an adequate development of Derry.

In the Republic political pressures favouring dispersed development prevented the emergence of any coherent growth centre policy throughout the 1960s, although such a policy was advocated in January, 1963, by the Committee on Industrial Organisation—a body established to survey the Republic's degree of preparedness for free trade; by a Committee on Development Centres and Industrial Estates (1964); and by the National Industrial Economic Council (1965); and the details of such a policy were worked out in the Buchanan Report, completed in 1968. While in practice a tendency towards more concentrated development manifested itself in the latter part of the 1960s, the Republic continued to suffer throughout this period from the effects of inadequate concentration of industrial development and the consequent absence of an adequate infrastructure for large-scale industrial development outside Dublin.

The expansion of industry in Northern Ireland was also facilitated by the exceptionally well-organised facilities for industrial training, a heritage of the war-time period when the relatively sheltered environment of Northern Ireland encouraged the development of industrial training facilities there. In the Republic, on the other hand, industrial training was neglected until the mid-1960s, when the establishment of a separate Department of Labour, and of an organisation working under the aegis of this department to develop industrial training facilities (ANCO), began, all too slowly, to fill this gap.

Economic development in the Republic was facilitated, however, throughout much of the period from 1922 onwards by an approach to the role of State industry which was notably less doctrinaire than that of the Northern Ireland Government. The conservatism of Ulster Unionism, frustrated in the field of social security by the need to move step by step with Britain in this field, was manifest in the cautious attitude adopted to the development of State enterprise. Although certain basic facilities in Northern Ireland are State-owned, e.g. the provision of electricity outside the two main cities, Belfast and Derry, rail transport, the bulk of road passenger transport and part of road freight transport—many activities undertaken by the State in the Republic have not developed at all in Northern Ireland— e.g. the exploitation of peat resources, the production of sugar from beet, or the production of steel, industrial alcohol, or nitrogenous fertilisers, or are undertaken by British concerns, e.g. the provision of air transport facilities and of shipping services, of life assurance, and of export promotion facilities. Industrial development, which in the Republic is organised through autonomous State concerns such as the Industrial Development Authority, the Industrial Credit Company and the Shannon Free Airport Development Company, is in Northern Ireland promoted directly by the Ministry of Commerce.

The relatively extensive development of State enterprise in the Republic does not reflect any greater acceptance of or enthusiasm for socialism South of the Border than North. The initiative taken in the Republic by the State in so many fields has not arisen from any ideological commitment to State as against private enterprise but rather from the need to fill certain gaps in a relatively under-developed economy, where some activities either failed to emerge through the initiatives of the private sector, or failed to survive after being started by private interests. It is fair to say, however, that in the Republic there has been no ideological reluctance to contemplate State activity in such cases; at least until the publication of an Economic Council Report on this subject in late 1971 this had been a feature of Northern Ireland. The governing party in Northern Ireland has always been closely linked to the British Conservative Party.

There has also been a subtle difference in attitudes to econ-

omic development in the two parts of Ireland. The subordinate
role of the Northern Ireland Government and Parliament has
encouraged the province to look towards Britain for aid in
many areas where the Republic has been forced to rely on its
own resources. The original meaning of Sinn Fein—standing on
one's own feet—has continued to have significance in the
Republic, where national self-reliance has grown during the
half-century of independence. It is at least arguable that the
opposite has happened in Northern Ireland, where the effect of
having a separate but subordinate system of government has
been to highlight the dependence of Northern Ireland on the
United Kingdom through subsidies, which in most cases are no
different from those that exist in peripheral areas of Great
Britain itself, where, however, they are hidden from sight
within the unitary system of government. By thus identifying
the high degree of dependence of Northern Ireland on Great
Britain, the system has tended to undermine to some degree the
traditional self-reliance of the Ulsterman during the past half-
century, thus helping to reverse the traditional contrast between
Northerners and Southerners in Ireland.

This was highlighted by the negotiations for entry to the
European Economic Community. The Republic as an independent State negotiated its own terms of entry into the Community, seeking and securing such adjustments to the terms of
the Treaty of Rome as were necessary to achieve a smooth transition to full membership. These negotiations were closely, and
critically, followed in the Republic, where, moreover, the issue
of membership had to be put to a referendum because of changes that membership made necessary to the Republic's written
Constitution.

Nothing similar happened in Northern Ireland. Northern
Ministers paid one visit to Brussels during the negotiations, but
this was a mission of information rather than a negotiating
exercise. Only one transitional provision was specially negotiated by the British Government for the benefit of Northern
Ireland—the temporary retention of the Safeguarding of Employment Act 1948, under which the Northern Ireland Government controls the employment in Northern Ireland of non-
residents. Neither the Government nor the people of the
Province had any say in whether it joined the Community or
not (apart from the votes of the province's twelve MPs at Westminster, a majority of whom opposed membership), and public

opinion in Northern Ireland remained apathetic throughout the period of negotiations—reflecting a sense of impotence that had a certain parallel also in Scotland.

In one sense all of the economic differences between North and South that have developed during the past fifty years are obstacles to reunion—when two parts of a country pursue such different paths for half-a-century, it must inevitably be more difficult to bring them together again. On the other hand few of these differences are insuperable, even in the relatively short run. The different patterns of industrial development, the competitive rather than complementary character of the two industrial economies, the somewhat different attitudes towards state enterprise, and the greater self-reliance of the Republic after half-a-century of political independence—none of these are really important. Only the problem posed by UK subsidies to Northern Ireland's agriculture—which will be largely solved by EEC membership—and to the Northern Ireland social services are real obstacles to reunion.

LIVING STANDARD COMPARISONS

There is clear evidence that material living standards are on average higher in Northern Ireland than the Republic. Figures for gross domestic product and for personal income in the two areas show that in 1969 average GDP per head in Northern Ireland was 18% higher than in the Republic (£494 as against £417); while personal income per head was almost 25% higher (£524 as against £422). Of course this comparison is valid only to the extent that the purchasing power of the pound is the same in the Republic as in Northern Ireland; but such comparisons as have been made between price levels in the Republic and Northern Ireland, or the Republic and the United Kingdom, suggest that prices in the Republic are in fact higher than in the North,[4] and this information is confirmed by common observation. To the extent that prices are higher on balance in the

[4] Professor Charles Carter read a paper to the Statistical and Social Enquiry Society of Ireland in December, 1954, on National Income and Social Accounts in Northern Ireland. In his research for this paper Professor Carter found that while in 1954 food prices in Belfast were $2\frac{1}{2}$% higher than in Dublin and drink and tobacco prices 35% higher, on the other hand the price of clothing was 20% lower, fuel and light was 20–25% lower, and household goods 7% lower. Between 1954 and 1961 the Consumer price index rose by 61% in the United Kingdom but by 72% in the Republic, which, if the prices of other goods and services were similar in Belfast and in

Republic, the difference in average material living standards indicated by the above comparisons of personal income per head would, of course, be correspondingly greater. In very broad terms it seems probable that average material living standards in Northern Ireland are over one-quarter higher than in the Republic.

How much of the difference in living standards between the Republic and Northern Ireland is directly attributable to the subsidies from the UK referred to above? If one leaves on one side the indirect subsidy involved in the relief from responsibility for financing defence, the remuneration of the national debt and the monarchy, as well as the benefits arising from the way in which taxes handed over by the UK Government are calculated, there remained in 1971/72 about £100 m. of direct additions to personal income in Northern Ireland, arising from agricultural subsidies, and UK subsidisation of social security provisions in Northern Ireland. This represented just over 10% of personal income in Northern Ireland in that year. Thus almost half of the difference between average per capita personal income in the two parts of Ireland in 1971/72 seems to have been directly attributable to the impact of UK subsidies on personal incomes in Northern Ireland.

The remainder of the difference in average income between the two parts of Ireland reflects a combination of different levels of income per head in agriculture, and to a lesser extent in the distribution, transport and communications sector, and, more important, perhaps, the different mix of employments in the two areas—with low-income agriculture looming much larger in the economy of the Republic than in that of Northern Ireland.

Dublin in 1954, would on a weighted average basis suggest that prices in Dublin in 1969 were fractionally higher than in Belfast.

However, price comparisons in respect of November, 1961, undertaken by Prof. Edward Nevin (*The Irish Price Level: A Conservative Study*, Paper No. 9, Economic Research Institute) suggested that in that year basic food prices were similar in the UK and the Republic, but prices of competitive goods were 7–8% lower in the UK and prices of goods not manufactured in Ireland were about 20% lower in the UK than in the Republic. Between November, 1961 and 1969 consumer prices rose by 31½% in the UK and by 42% in the Republic—which suggests that by 1969 a significant price difference may have existed between the two countries. Assuming that prices in Northern Ireland were reasonably close to the UK average, this would indicate a significantly higher price level in the Republic than in Northern Ireland in 1969.

In 1953, income per head in agriculture for self-employed persons, employers and relatives assisting was 85% higher in Northern Ireland than in the Republic and in the non-agricultural sector for the same non-employee group the disparity was about 70%. By contrast the differentials for employees were 42% in agriculture, 8% in distribution, $1\frac{1}{2}$% in industry and 27% in other sectors. But for a 23% differential in employee incomes in the metal and engineering group, partly accounted for by a smaller proportion of women workers in Northern Ireland, the average income per industrial employee in Northern Ireland would have been lower in money terms in 1953 than in the Republic. These comparisons are based on Professor Carter's private estimates for Northern Ireland which were more detailed than the official estimates now available for national income and expenditure in the area.[5]

A comparison of the official employment and national accounts figures for the two areas in 1969 (the latest year for which full figures are available), shows a somewhat similar pattern to that revealed by the 1953 study. Average output per head in agriculture, including employees as well as self-employed, was 65% higher in Northern Ireland than in the Republic in that year. (The equivalent figure for 1953 was a 73% differential for the agricultural sector as a whole.) Average output per person engaged in industry was almost identical in the two areas in 1969—£1,370 in Northern Ireland and £1,360 in the Republic—closely paralleling the virtual identity of average employee income in this sector in 1953. Output per person engaged in distribution, transport, communications and finance in 1969 was about 20% higher in Northern Ireland than in the Republic. This compares with an 8% differential in favour of Northern Ireland in income per employee in the distribution sector in 1953. On the other hand the marked differential in other employee incomes in favour of Northern Ireland which emerged from the 1953 study finds no parallel in the 1969 figures, which show average income per head about one-third higher in the Republic in the public administration and defence sector, and a fractional margin in favour of the Republic in the residual sector of the economy—professions, etc. Whereas in 1953 average income per person gainfully employed was 27% higher in Northern Ireland than in the Repub-

[5] Details of these calculations will be found in 'The Irish Economy North and South', by Garret FitzGerald, *Studies*, Winter 1956.

lic, in 1969 it was only 18% higher. But this narrowing of income differences was probably approximately offset by a faster increase in prices in the Republic, so that the gap in living standards between the two areas may not have been much different in 1969 from what it had been in 1953.

How significant is an income difference of this magnitude? Is it within the normal range of income differences with unitary States? The answer to this latter question is quite clearly in the affirmative. Thus in Italy in 1965 the net domestic product per capita of the greater part of the country was about 75% higher than that of the South. Even in a small country like the Netherlands in the same year income per head in the country as a whole was 22% higher than in the poorest province. And in Germany the seven better-off regions had an average per capita net domestic product more than 20% above that of the four poorest provinces.[6]

Moreover within the Republic itself income differences exist that are as great as those between the Republic and Northern Ireland. Thus East Leinster (viz. the region comprising the eight counties of Louth, Meath, Dublin, Kildare, Carlow, Kilkenny, Wicklow and Wexford) which has an area close to that of Northern Ireland (3.17 m. acres as against 3.35 m. acres) and a population not much less than that of Northern Ireland (estimated at 1,287,000 in 1969 as compared with 1,512,000 in Northern Ireland), had estimated per capita personal income of about £500 in 1969—20% above the national average, and 40% above the average for the remainder of the Republic. Indeed the level of average personal income in East Leinster in 1969 was only 5% below that of Northern Ireland, which in 1969 is estimated to have been about £526 per head.[7]

There is thus little to choose between the North-East and South-East of the island of Ireland so far as incomes and living standards are concerned; in terms of income arising in the region the South-East probably had in 1969 a slightly higher level, indeed, than the North-East. Through an accident of history the South-East is, however, linked politically to the much poorer Midlands and West, whereas the North-East has cut itself off successfully from these less prosperous areas of Ireland,

[6] See article by Garret FitzGerald, *Irish Times*, based on tables in Appendix to EEC Regional Policy, 1969.

[7] Irish County Incomes, 1969, Michael Ross, Economic and Social Research Institute Paper, 1972.

and is politically linked to Great Britain. As a result, whereas the South-East has to 'carry' the Midlands and West, transferring substantial sums to them in various forms, thus *reducing* its living standards, the North-East is a recipient of subsidies from Great Britain, which *raised* its standard of living in 1969 slightly above that of the South-East.

5. The Religious Issue

THE attention given to economic factors in the preceding chapters should not mislead anyone into under-estimating the importance of the religious element in the Irish problem. While economic factors certainly underlay the drifting apart of North and South before 1920, and while important economic differences now represent real obstacles to unity, the most fundamental obstacle to a peaceful reunification is the sense of distinctness that is felt by a large proportion of Protestants in Northern Ireland—a feeling of not belonging to the rest of the Irish community, with whom they share the island of Ireland.

The differentiation between this group and the rest of the people of the island is not, of course, purely a religious one. For one thing Protestants in the Republic have largely come to share a sense of common national identity with Catholics in this part of Ireland; for the most part they feel themselves to be Irish rather than British, although this does not exclude a sense on the part of some of them of a special relationship with Britain. Again in Northern Ireland itself there is—and has been for several centuries—a minority of Protestants who feel themselves to be Irish rather than members of a separate group distinct from the Irish nation. But it is fair to say that the sense of a separate identity is almost completely confined to Protestants, and to-day to Protestants in Northern Ireland for the most part. The core of the problem lies amongst this group.

The origins of this sense of distinctness have been traced in the introductory, historical chapter. The most important single factor that prevented the settlers in the north-east from becoming absorbed into the general Irish culture as earlier settlers had become absorbed, was the obstacle to inter-marriage posed by the religious differences between them and the rest of the Irish people. The strength of the feeling between the bulk of Ulster Protestants and Catholics finds its roots in the religious wars of the seventeenth century, but the survival of this bitterness through three centuries and a half has depended on the maintenance of the distinction between the two communities in Ulster—and this has been due above all to the absence of inter-marriage. It is the fact that marriages between the two communities have been so rare that has prevented the blurring of distinctions that might otherwise have occurred; the lack of inter-marriage has also preserved very largely the racial purity of the Ulster Scots, and, more important, still, their sense of being a race apart.

It is, of course, only an accident of history that the factor that has maintained the distinction between the Ulster Scots and the native Irish in Ulster has been a religious one. In other parts of the world differences of colour or clear-cut racial differences, or differences of language lie at the root of the differentiation between different communities living more or less side by side, but separately in the same region. But because the racial differences between Ulster Scots and Irish were not at any time clearly distinguishable to the eye, and because throughout almost the whole of Ulster the native Irish abandoned the Irish language in favour of English in the eighteenth and nineteenth centuries, the two races would have become almost completely assimilated had it not been for the accident of their religious differences and the obstacle this posed to inter-marriage. There might have remained, perhaps, some vestiges of differences in forms of agriculture practised, as are said to exist still between Normans and Celts in South Wexford, or between German Palatines and Irish in Limerick, but little more.

But while the fact that religion is the dividing element between the two communities in Northern Ireland is a historical accident, and while it is true to say that the inter-community conflict in Northern Ireland is not a religious war, in the sense of a war about religious dogmas, it would be a mistake to under-estimate the underlying importance of the divergence in atti-tude of Protestants and Catholics on a number of issues of fundamental importance to the running of a State. The North-ern Protestants' fears of Catholicism, which largely stand in the way of a united Ireland, stem from what Protestants see as the claim of the Catholic Church to influence State policy on mat-ters which Protestants regard as outside the proper sphere of church authority. In particular the Catholic Church's claims in the educational sphere, in medicine, and in matters of public morality are seen as impinging on what many Protestants regard as their liberties. Catholics, on the other hand, accustomed to the claims of their Church to ensure the passing on of its teaching through control of education, and to secure the enforcement of private morality by State action, are tempted to see the Protestant attitude to these matters as lax or permissive. And just as Northern Protestants have found some of their prejudices about Catholicism confirmed by the way in which the independent Irish State south of the Border has run its affairs during the first half-century of its existence, so also Catholics, in the South perhaps rather more than in the North, are prone to feel that their more authoritarian attitudes are vindicated by the development of a permissive society in Great Britain, with which, it must be said, most Southern Catholics are much more familiar than with Northern Ireland!

'Protestant attitudes towards Catholicism are, however, much more important in this context than Catholic attitudes towards Protestantism. The Irish problem is quite simply the fruit of Northern Protestant reluctance to become part of what they regard as an authoritarian Southern Catholic State. This is the obstacle to be overcome. It is *their* fears that have to be resolved if tensions in the North are to be eased, and Ireland is to be united. It is true that this will pose problems for the Catholic majority in the Republic—problems of adjustment to a pluralist society—but this is a second and, hopefully, less difficult stage in the affair, and one that in any event cannot be successfully tackled until the precise nature of Protestant fears is understood.

It may be felt that in expressing the problem in religious terms, and in appearing to exclude the question of Northern Protestant loyalty to Britain, an important element is being overlooked, or at any rate under-played. It is arguable, however, that Northern Protestant loyalty to Britain, to the extent that it exists, is an accidental by-product of the religious and economic issues, rather than an issue in its own right. It is true that the traditional and formal expression of the Northern Protestant attitude has been in terms of loyalty to Britain, and it could also be argued that a colony so close to the homeland could retain a genuine sense of still belonging to the 'mother country', which more distant colonies almost invariably seem to lose, unless they are very small indeed, like Gibraltar, or like the islands of Martinique or Guadeloupe in the West Indies. But looking beneath the surface of events, there is evidence to be found which suggests the contrary—that Northern Protestant loyalty to Britain is not a fundamental issue.

First of all, until the 'threat' of Catholic Emancipation loomed large, Irish Protestant attitudes tended to favour a measure of independence of Britain, whose all-too-evident efforts to exploit its Irish colony in the eighteenth century created a resentment amongst Irish Protestants not dissimilar to that felt by the Protestant inhabitants of New England about the same time. Moreover, the Northern Dissenters in Ireland, who in the eighteenth century suffered, although less severely than Catholics, from the Penal Laws, demonstrated their resentment against Britain in a very concrete way during the Rebellion of 1798. Thus whatever loyalty Irish Protestants may originally have felt towards their mother-country had worn pretty thin by the end of the eighteenth century. The apparent revival of this loyalty in the nineteenth century can thus be seen to have been a rather artificial growth; Irish Protestants began to look again towards Britain when they felt their Protestant 'liberties'—or privileges—threatened by the rising tide of Catholic Emancipation. Lord Randolph Churchill may have decided to play the Orange card in the 1880s, but Irish Protestants had already started to play the British card for their own benefit more than half a century earlier.

Evidence for this thesis is not, however, confined to past centuries, *vide* the willingness of Northern Protestants in 1912–1914 to contemplate armed rebellion against the British Crown to prevent the operation of a Home Rule Bill which, even if it had not contained an exclusion clause for the six north-eastern counties, would have still left them subjects of the Crown with representation in the UK Parliament. No clearer evidence than that could be needed for the thesis that in this century the corner-stone of Northern Protestant thinking is a rejection of participation in an Irish State with a Catholic majority, rather than desire to remain loyal subjects of the Crown.

Towards the end of the 1960s, as the Civil Rights protests provoked counter-reactions and as the North slid into near-civil war, the spirit of 1912–1914 found fresh expression.

Finally, towards the end of 1971, the extreme Protestant leaders, Rev. Ian Paisley and Desmond Boal, gave expression in press briefings—and, in the case of the former, in more muted press and radio interviews also—to their fundamental concern with what they regard as Protestant rights, whose safeguarding they clearly regard as taking precedence over the political connection with the UK. For the moment they and other like-minded Protestants still see participation in the UK as their best hope of maintaining these 'liberties', but they have made it clear—understandably by implication rather than by explicit statement—that they would not necessarily exclude participation in a united Ireland if these 'liberties' could be secured, and that their loyalty to Britain is conditional rather than absolute.

It is important that this fundamental element in Northern Protestant 'grass-roots' thinking be understood. The flamboyant expressions of loyalty to the Crown, and generous use of the United Kingdom flag as a party symbol, can give a quite misleading impression of what lies at the root of Northern Unionist attitudes. Of course for the great mass of not-very-deep-thinking Protestants in the North, no distinction between loyalty to Britain and the preservation of Protestant 'freedoms' is seen, much less admitted. Moreover, there are many Protestants, probably more in the middle classes than amongst the working-class, who have a genuine and positive loyalty to Britain, expressed in some families by a tradition of service in the British defence forces. But deep down in the typical Protestant Ulsterman, 'Protestant rights' come before any loyalty to the neighbouring island, and under the pressure of the events of 1968 onwards this underlying feeling has come increasingly to the surface, evidenced by the growing use of the Ulster flag—little known before 1969—as an adjunct to or even alternative to the Union Jack.

The growth of what might be described as Ulster Protestant nationalism in recent years, encouraged by what many Northern Protestants feel to have been a lack of understanding and sympathy with their plight on the part of people and politicians in Britain, has been paralleled by a diminution of British interest in the retention of Northern Ireland within the United Kingdom. Even before the events of the years from 1968 onwards started to generate a distaste in many British minds for continued involvement in and responsibility for the affairs of Northern Ireland, the political and strategic reasons which had once made the retention of Northern Ireland as part of the UK seem mandatory, had begun to weaken. For British strategists

Northern Ireland is now a liability rather than an asset; it is seen as making demands on British military strength, rather than as adding to the potential wartime effectiveness of British forces. Irish nationalists, for long nurtured on the thesis that the continuance of Partition reflected British determination to retain an important military base on Irish soil, must now reconsider this theory and begin to face the fact that the reunification of Ireland is now genuinely an Irish problem, and an Irish problem alone. Britain has no longer any interest in standing in the way of a peaceful reunification of Ireland; indeed, she has every interest in promoting such an outcome, which would relieve her Exchequer and cut her military liabilities significantly.

Thus while many Northern Protestants still feel themselves to be influenced by sentiments of loyalty to Britain, and while Britain's political leaders have been slow to reverse engines and to start to advocate positively the reunification of Ireland and the ending of Northern Ireland's ties with Britain, it is now evident that the British connection is no longer the crucial factor in the Irish problem. The issue now is whether and how the fears of the Northern Protestant majority about their role within a United Ireland, in which Catholics would have a three-to-one majority, can be allayed.

The calming of these fears is obviously important as a preliminary to reunification; but it is not only in that context that it is important. Because so much of the internal tension in Northern Ireland has arisen from fear—in the first instance Protestant fears of being forced into a Catholic-dominated United Ireland, and secondarily Catholic fears of Protestant pogroms—anything that allays fear will help to reduce tension and facilitate peaceful relations between the two communities in Northern Ireland. Moreover as the prospect of an eventual reunification becomes increasingly accepted as a real one, however reluctantly in the case of many Northern Protestants, the need for reassurance as to the terms of such an ultimate national unity becomes all the greater.

It is against this background that at the end of 1971 politicians in the Republic belatedly started to discuss changes in the present Constitution and laws of that State designed to meet legitimate fears of Northern Protestants and legitimate grievances of Protestants in the South. That any such changes must necessarily be provisional in character (in the sense of being incomplete, but, of course, guaranteed), leaving it to an eventual united Irish people to devise a new Constitution appropriate to their needs, was, of course, fully recognised. Indeed some of the reluctance expressed by the Taoiseach, Mr. Lynch, concerning this work of revision may have been due to fears on his part that by proposing changes in the present Constitution at a time when reunification is not an immediate issue, it might be thought that these changes were intended to produce a Constitution to be accepted by the people of Northern Ireland without further change.

The problem of meeting Northern Protestant fears cannot, however, be tackled by constitutional and legal changes alone. The objections of Northern Protestants to reunification with the Republic derive as much from the way in which its institutions have operated in practice as from its Constitution and laws. Moreover, on one point at least, and a very important one, Protestant objections go outside the competence of the Republic's political leaders; the problem posed by the *Ne Temere* decree on mixed marriages, which has been responsible for a significant part of the decline in the Protestant population of the Republic, is one that can be resolved only by the authorities of the Catholic Church.

Moreover changes in the Republic's Constitution and laws will not satisfy Northern Protestants if they continue to feel, and are given reason to feel, that in a United Ireland the Catholic majority will still be influenced by what Protestants see as an authoritarian desire to enforce private morality by means of public law. This problem lies at the root of the whole matter, and its resolution is not made any easier by the fact that the Protestant position in this matter is not internally consistent. In Northern Ireland and Great Britain, as probably, in every other country, the State intervenes in matters of private morality which it sees as affecting public order. The fact that the British and Northern Ireland laws on divorce are relatively 'liberal' does not mean that the regulation of marriage, and of its termination, by law does not involve an intrusion of the State into matters of private morality. The fact that the British and Northern Ireland film censorship is 'liberal' in comparison with that in the Republic does not mean that the principle of censorship is not accepted and applied in the United Kingdom. The fact that the law on obscenity in the United Kingdom is not enforced as rigidly as it used to be does not affect the fact that such a law exists. Absolute freedom in matters of morality is not permitted by the law of the United Kingdom, or of any other country, and the differences between the legal position on such matters in Northern Ireland and in the Republic is one of degree rather than one of principle. And being a matter of degree, it is necessarily a matter of opinion.

It is certainly true that the fact that much more 'liberal' legislation on such matters exists in the United Kingdom, and is acceptable to the relatively puritanical Protestant people of Northern Ireland, reflects a difference in approach vis-à-vis the Republic that is influenced by the Protestant ethic as it currently finds expression in Britain and Northern Ireland. But, even leaving on one side the fact that in the past Protestant countries have been more repressive than Catholic countries in matters of morality—and that some still are, e.g. the laws of some New England States against contraception or of other American States in respect of adultery—the difference in degree between the Protestant-inspired approach in the UK and the Catholic-inspired approach in the Republic of Ireland, does not provide a very clear-cut basis for formulating a new approach to such legislation.

To some Catholics, especially in the Republic, the insistence of Northern Protestants on these 'rights' suggests support for a permissive society, and it is sometimes argued that as most Northern Protestants are known to be highly moral people, they cannot conceivably want such rights, and are therefore not serious in seeking them. This interpretation betrays an inability to understand the Protestant attitude to such matters, however. Although in practice Protestants accept much moral legislation, they tend to be much more hostile than Catholics to the enforcement of private morality by law. Thus most Protestants who disapprove of the re-marriage of divorced people—and this has been the official attitude of the Church of Ireland, and one shared by many members of that Church—nevertheless believe that a human right of civil divorce exists, and that it would be wrong to deny such a remedy to people who do not feel debarred by religious scruples from engaging in divorce proceedings with a view to re-marriage. Moreover, even Protestants who do not approve of, or practice, artificial methods of contraception regard the right to do so as fundamental. And, despite general acceptance of the practice of censorship in the cinema and of the practice of prosecuting the publishers or purveyors of obscene literature, almost all Protestants reject the concept of an advance censorship of books.

Catholics may argue that in some at least of these attitudes Protestants are either internally inconsistent, or have no firm philosophical basis for the distinctions they make. Catholics may also argue that their own approach towards some of these issues is sociologically and psychologically sound, and that the Protestant approach ignores the importance of opportunity in relation to deviations from sexual morality, or that the corrosive effects especially on young people of public displays of obscenity are greatly under-estimated by Protestant opponents of censorship, for example. Such arguments miss the point, however. The matters in question are for Protestants, and above all for Northern Irish Protestants, symbols of what they regard as a fundamental difference in approach between Catholics and themselves, and they do not wish to belong to a society in which the moral consensus of a Catholic majority prevails on these and other related issues, rather than considerations of the general welfare of the whole community, Protestant as well as Catholic.

At another level, Northern Protestants fear the general influence of the Catholic Church on State policies, and believe that in the Republic their fears are amply justified. Article 44 of the Constitution, with its ambiguous reference to the special position of the Catholic Church as the guardian of the faith of the majority of the Irish people, symbolises all that Protestants fear, but the mere removal of this article will not necessarily reassure Northern Protestants. They are not naive enough to believe that the influence the Catholic Church has exerted on legislation in the Republic has derived from this Article of the Constitution. They believe rather that the acceptance by the mass of Catholics in the Republic of what Protestants regard as the authoritarian attitude of the Catholic Church on many matters of public policy lies at the root of the problem. The mere removal of this article of the Constitution will not necessarily convince them that within a united Irish State, in which Catholics would still form 75% of the electorate, laws would not still be devised along lines conforming to the views of the Catholic ecclesiastical authorities, accepted by their flock.

This is a much more difficult problem to tackle than constitutional or legislative changes. What is involved is a question of trust and confidence, which can be built up only over a period of time, during which the Catholic majority in the Republic give solid evidence of a willingness—even a determination—to ensure that legislation on sensitive matters would be along lines acceptable to the Protestant minority, and not just along lines that commend themselves to the Catholic majority.

Many Catholics find this hard to accept. The same words that have been used by many Unionists during the years since 1968—'the majority has *some* rights, after all'—spring to many Catholic lips in the Republic when any proposal is made along the lines outlined in the previous paragraph.

It is this dilemma that lies at the root of the Irish problem. If the Protestant minority in the North is to be persuaded that participation in a united Ireland will involve guarantees for what they regard as their 'freedoms' and their 'rights', a sustained—and guaranteed—effort of self-abnegation on the part of the Catholic majority will be called for, and a willingness to refrain from legislating in accordance with the instincts of this majority and with what the majority could legitimately regard as its 'right'.

Doubts about the willingness of the Catholic majority in the Republic to make such a sacrifice are not, perhaps, confined to the Northern Protestants. The Government in the Republic, by its refusal to allow private members' bills on contraception a first reading in the Senate in 1971, and the Dail in February, 1972, and by its attempt in 1971 also to enforce a form of 'community school' acceptable to the Catholic hierarchy but unacceptable to the Protestant school authorities, has also seemed to reflect doubts on this score.

It is not really surprising that first reactions in the Republic to this very real problem posed by the concept of reunion by consent have been so hesitant and uncertain. As was suggested in Chapter 3, one of the unfortunate by-products of Partition was the evolution of the independent Irish State along lines that were far from 'pluralist' and that could not by any stretch of imagination be visualised as likely to be acceptable to Northern Protestants. Over a period of fifty years most Catholics in the Republic became attuned to a state of things in which the shape of controversial legislation was largely determined by Catholic thinking—though with some conscious efforts to limit consequent unfairness to the small Protestant community. Partition on the other hand became for most people in the Republic, during most of this period, a matter of slogans—and a very unreal issue at that.

It is not easy for the people of the Republic after so long a conditioning to break away and to adopt overnight a liberal, pluralist approach to these matters. There is a natural tendency to say, 'not yet, O Lord, not yet', like the sinner called to repentance. Years of sloganeering about Partition have made it more difficult for people to face the realities of the problem, and the constant reiteration over fifty years of the idea that the Republic has a 'right' to Northern Ireland, has tended to dull sensitivities on the critical issues. If the Republic has a 'right' to the North, many Southern Catholics ask, why should it have to turn its way of life inside out to accommodate a minority of the Irish people—and a recalcitrant minority at that?

In seeking to understand Northern Protestant attitudes we have the advantage of the results of a very comprehensive social survey carried out in 1968, just before the Derry march that launched the troubles in the North. This survey has been published and very fully analysed by Professor Richard Rose, in his book, *Governing Without Consensus*.[1] Of particular interest are the contrasts between the Protestant and Catholic communities in Northern Ireland as they emerge from this study.

First of all, despite the fact that the 'under-dog' position of Catholics in Northern Ireland, and their more authoritarian religion, might have been expected to make them narrower and more insecure and unsettled than their Protestant neighbours, the opposite proved to be the case.

Thus Protestant respondents reported that in their youth their parents had been less favourable to mixing between Protestants and Catholics—16% being against as compared with 9% in the case of Catholics, and 35% in favour as against 43% in the case of Catholics. Protestants were also more likely to have had a 'ghetto' background—57% reported they had been brought up in areas that were mostly Protestant whereas only 38% of Catholics said they had been brought up in areas that were mostly Catholic; and whereas 46% of Catholics had been brought up in mixed areas, this was true of only 34% of Protestants.

Whereas over half of the 41% of Protestants who belonged to clubs or organisations belonged to exclusively Protestant institutions, barely a quarter of the 19% of Catholics who reported such membership belonged to all-Catholic clubs, and while

[1] Richard Rose, *Governing Without Consensus*, Faber and Faber, 1971.

only 3% of Catholics were members of the Ancient Order of Hibernians, 19% of Protestants were Orangemen.

Twice as many Protestants as Catholics felt that the past could not be ignored in Northern Ireland (20% as against 9%). More Protestants (35% as against 26%) felt that to cross party lines and vote with the other side would make a big difference with their friends and family, and barely half as many (11% as against 21%) felt it would make no difference. Protestants were also more prone to believe that it was important to bring up children to have the same views as their parents on the Border question and to vote the same way as their parents (25–27% as against 16–17%). And 69% of Protestants would have disapproved of legislation against religious discrimination in employment or housing, while almost half of those expressing a view on the issue would have approved Government measures to prevent Catholic influence from growing stronger.

The 'siege mentality' betrayed by these answers was also reflected in the replies to questions about the use of force. Whereas only 60% of Catholics felt it had been right for people in the South to take up arms fifty years earlier and fight in order to make a Republic, 82% of Protestants felt it had been right for people in the North in 1912–1914 to take up arms and stand ready to fight to keep Northern Ireland British. Moreover this disparity in attitudes to the use of force was even more striking in relation to the present—whereas only 13% of Catholics agreed with the proposition that it would be right to take any measures necessary in order to end Partition and bring Ulster into the Republic, 52% of Protestants felt that it would be right to take any measures necessary in order to keep Northern Ireland a Protestant area.

The harder attitudes of Protestants on these issues was, however, accompanied by a greater uncertainty about national identity, and a somewhat greater feeling of unsettledness. Thus slightly less Protestants than Catholics would be 'very unhappy' if they had to leave Northern Ireland. And whereas over three-quarters of Catholics described themselves as 'Irish', Protestants were much more divided on this issue—39% saying they were British, 32% 'Ulster' and 20% Irish. It is also interesting in this connection to note evidence of a slight inter-generational shift in attitudes on the Protestant side—the figure of 39% of Protestants describing themselves as British compared with 46% who said their parents had described themselves as

British, and the 32% who considered themselves to be Ulster-men was a somewhat bigger proportion than the 27% who said their parents thought of themselves in this way.

Protestants were less inclined to go to Church—35% said they never, or hardly ever, did so, as against 3% of Catholics; and the number who attended weekly or more often was only 46% in the case of Protestants as against 95% for Catholics. Protestants, moreover, were much less ecumenical than Catho-lics—60% thought the unity of the Catholic and Protestant churches would be undesirable, whereas 69% of Catholics thought it would be desirable. Moreover whereas 72% of Protestants thought church unity impossible, only 41% of Catholics held this view.

Finally, Protestants were significantly better off than Catho-lics—18% had family incomes in excess of £30 per week in 1968, as against only 8% of Catholics, and whereas 66% of Catholics had incomes below £20 per week, this was true of only 53% of Protestants. (There is other evidence, incidentally, of income differences within the Protestant community, be-tween Church of Ireland members and Presbyterians—to the disadvantage of the former.) The picture of the Northern Protestant community and its attitudes that emerges from this survey is not one calculated to encourage those who favour a united Ireland—and it must be remembered that this 'snap-shot' of the Northern Protestant is one taken in 1968, *before* the troubles began. The events of the years from 1968 onwards are unlikely to have done much to soften the harsh outlines of this picture.

As was mentioned earlier, however, these years have seen a growth of Ulster nationalism, and a growing disillusionment with Britain's role in the affairs of Northern Ireland. If such a survey were taken again to-day it seems possible that the pro-portion of Protestants describing themselves as 'Ulstermen' and 'Ulsterwomen' would be significantly higher than in 1968—at the expense, probably, of both the 'British' and 'Irish' identifi-cations of that year. In the long run this may have considerable significance; few in Ulster believe that such a small community could stand on its own in the modern world and as the sense of 'Britishness' diminishes, and the sense of an Ulster identity grows, the possibility may emerge of an eventual more rational approach to the question of its relationship with the rest of the people on the island of Ireland. But this can come about only if the people of the Republic become fully sensitive to the fears and aspirations of Northern Protestants, and decide to make the changes in their own community that will calm these fears and give assurance that these aspirations can be accommodated within a united Ireland.

How this might best be done will be considered in a later chapter. At this stage it will be enough to point out that the choice facing the people of the Republic is a difficult one—that of substituting a pluralist society for a largely Catholic-orientated one, or else giving up hope of a peaceful reunification of Ireland just at the time when this is beginning to appear again to be a possibility. It is made the more difficult because it is a choice that can all too easily be blurred or fudged. Thus there are those who believe that the North can be bombed into a united Ireland; there are those who believe that Britain will do this dirty work for Ireland by pressurising the North into a united Ireland similar to the kind of State that already exists in the Republic; and there are those who will simply refuse to face the choice because they feel it to be such an awkward one, and who will therefore keep their heads firmly embedded in the sand.

The dilemma is, of course, most acute for the institutional Catholic Church. The influence which church authorities have exercised in the independent Irish State throughout most of its existence has been considerable; John Whyte's book *Church and State in Modern Ireland* provides ample evidence for this. It cannot be easy for such an institution to surrender this influence willingly, given the rooted belief of many churchmen, especially of the older generation, that this influence is necessary to ensure the greater glory of God within the confines of the independent Irish State. The adjustment to a different society in which the institutional Church's role in public policy would be much more peripheral—and much less unique—would be a painful one for the ecclesiastical authorities concerned. Yet it is one that they may prove prepared to make, for more than one reason. First, as time passes, an increasing number of the clergy, and latterly also some members, of the Hierarchy, have begun to question the wisdom and the utility of the kind of influence on State policy hitherto exercised by the Catholic Church in Ireland. There is something of a generation gap here —but one that is steadily being closed as the years pass. It is no longer necessarily true that, as has been asserted in the past, consecration converts liberal priests into conservative bishops.

Secondly, the Catholic Church in Ireland is an all-Ireland institution, with its capital in Northern Ireland. A significant proportion of the bishops and priests are Northern Catholics, and the vast majority are nationalist in outlook, and as Irishmen they wish to see Ireland united, and any obstacles to such unity removed.

The willingness of the Catholic Church in Ireland, led by Cardinal Conway, himself a Belfastman, to accept and even welcome the proposed deletion from Article 44 of the Constitution of the reference to the 'special position' of the Catholic Church has already provided evidence for this, and although churchmen—including Cardinal Conway himself—opposed changes in the law on contraception when these were first seriously proposed in 1971, as well as opposing a change in the constitutional provisions banning divorce, this opposition was in a number of cases expressed to be only against making such a change *before* the issue of reunification seriously arose. Cardinal Conway, for example, specifically left open the question of what changes in these provisions might be made in the context of reunification.

A much more sensitive area is that of education, where the Catholic Church in Ireland has always strongly supported religious segregation. Nothing that has been said by the Cardinal or by any bishop offers a prospect of a change in attitude on this matter. This is, of course, a somewhat less crucial issue than the others in the context of reunification as many Protestants share the concern of the Catholic Church in Ireland for the preservation of a segregated educational system, especially members of the Church of Ireland, this attitude being reinforced by the effects of the *Ne Temere* decree upon mixed marriages that might arise from social intercourse between Protestants and Catholics starting in the schools. In Northern Ireland itself the educational system is largely segregated, although it is true that the Presbyterian Church has tended to favour integrated education. As the ending of segregated education is not pressed by most Protestants in the North, educational segregation in the Republic is not likely to be a major bone of contention, although many people of all religions concerned at the inter-community bitterness that exists in Northern Ireland, have come to feel that desegregation of education is desirable as a step towards diminishing these tensions.

What could have become a major issue, however, was the move made in 1971 to start merging the publicly-owned undenominational vocational schools with religious secondary schools in new 'community schools' to be in Catholic ownership and managed in a manner that would give a predominant voice to the Catholic religious orders involved. Clearly this development was incompatible with any attempt to persuade Protestants and especially Presbyterians, to accept participation in a United Ireland, for whatever preference many Protestants may have individually for segregated education, they resent deeply the proposed elimination of the inter-denominational public authority schools which at present provide a minority of Protestants with acceptable local education in rural areas where there are no Protestant schools, and an alternative type of education throughout the country. Moreover, the way in which this matter was organised by means of private consultations between the Department of Education and members of the Catholic Hierarchy, to the exclusion of any consultations with Protestant school authorities, grossly alienated Protestant opinion in the Republic.

This problem—a late and unnecessary complication in an already complex situation—has, however, largely been overcome as a result of the radical changes in the proposals made by the Minister under pressure from the political opposition and the Protestant Churches. As a result, there may now be no insuperable obstacle to a modification of attitude by the Catholic Church authorities to accommodate Protestant sensitivities, painful though this may be for some Catholic clergy and laity. There is room for agreement on these issues, and a strong motivation towards such agreement exists amongst Catholic churchmen, who would not wish to appear to stand in the way of the achievement of reunification by consent, should this become a real possibility.

6. The Impact of EEC Membership

THE obstacles to reunification are obvious enough from what has been said in preceding chapters. Despite the fact that the Protestant community in the Republic has been free from any repression or conscious discrimination throughout the history of the independent Irish State, the original hostility of Northern Protestant opinion to reunification has been strengthened rather than weakened by what it has seen of the evolution of this State since 1922. The neo-Gaelic and Catholic atmosphere of the Republic which its small Protestant minority has never attempted to challenge, offers no attraction to the dominant Protestant majority in the North—quite the reverse. To Southern Protestants these features of life in the Republic which began to emerge in the 1920s were of limited importance beside what many of them had feared would be their fate in an independent Irish State with a 94% Catholic majority, whereas to Northern Protestants, accustomed to living in a value-system of their own devising, the condition of Protestants in the Republic appears totally unacceptable.

Moreover, throughout the past half-century new obstacles have been raised to reunion—most notably, perhaps, the economic obstacle of the massive UK subsidies to the Northern Ireland economy, which contribute significantly to the higher living standards of Northern Ireland by comparison with the Republic.

Worst of all, perhaps, has been the violence of the period since 1969 which it must be said has made many Northern Protestants feel, however irrationally, that their worst suspicions of the Catholic minority in Northern Ireland were justi-

fied and has hardened their hearts against any closer links
between the North and the Republic. The conviction of so
many Northern Protestants that the Government of the Republic has failed to tackle the IRA within its jurisdiction and has
thus permitted or even connived at hostile incursions into
Northern Ireland from across the Border, has had a particularly
adverse effect on the attitudes of this section of the Northern
Ireland people towards the South.

Against this discouraging background what hopeful tenden-
cies can be detected, that might lead in time to the removal or
at any rate weakening, of some of these psychological or economic obstacles to reunification?

Membership of the European Communities may well prove
to be the most important single factor influencing events in a
positive direction in the years ahead—and this for a multiplicity of reasons. Some other factors may also be at work, however, favouring an eventual unification of the country, and these
merit a reference before considering in more detail the possible
impact of EEC membership.

First, there is the anachronistic character of the whole issue.
In Europe outside Northern Ireland, and indeed in many
other parts of the world, cultural differences based on religion
have gradually ceased to be seriously divisive factors within
societies. In part this reflects a decline in religious belief, which
not alone makes these cultural differences irrelevant for those
who cease to believe and practice the religion of their fore-
fathers, but which also tends to create amongst those who remain believing Christians a growing sense of Christian soli-
darity against neo-paganism. The sectarian differences of the
past have come to seem increasingly irrelevant to Christians in
many European countries as these Christians have become an
embattled minority, more conscious of what they share in common than of what divides them.

This trend has made remarkably little visible progress in the
exceptionally stony soil of Northern Ireland, or even in the less
polarised Republic, but this part of Europe cannot remain
indefinitely cut off from the forces at work elsewhere in the
world. The fact that by 1968 one-third of Northern Protestants
had ceased effectively to practice their religion, and that this
trend is presumably likely to continue in the years ahead, must
in time give rise to a new cleavage, between Christians and
non-Christians, which may eventually come to seem a lot more

relevant and important than the traditional Protestant/Catholic confrontation. It cannot even be excluded that one day the Orange Order may become a genuinely religious organisation, helping to keep alive the religious faith of Protestants rather than sectarian bitterness between Protestant and Catholic.

The growth of a more liberal Catholicism and of ecumenism in the Republic must also make its contribution. In the less polarised religious climate of the South closer relations between the different religious communities are easier to foster, and ecumenism has been less prone to be nipped by the frost of sectarianism. The emergence of a liberal and genuinely pluralist Christian society in the Republic, of which there are signs and harbingers, must in time dash the suspicions and weaken the fears of Northern Protestants about their likely fate in a united Ireland; nothing else can do so.

In this context it is worth commenting that, in the Republic especially, young people who are benefiting from, or have benefited from, further education have shown much less disposition to sympathise with or support extremist organisations than has been the case in the past. The universities have their Republican Clubs, but up to the early months of 1972, however, there was little sign in the Republic of significant active support for Republicanism in the universities on the scale that marked the 1940s, and even the late 1950s. Most students appeared very unattracted by the violence of the IRA. In Queens University, too, the students seemed less involved, and somewhat less polarised, than in the rest of the Northern community, although towards the end of 1971 a greater degree of polarisation seemed to be developing there.

Turning to the possible effects of EEC membership, although it would be quite wrong to look to this as a panacea for the Irish problem, which will always remain one to be settled by Irishmen in Ireland, such influence as membership of the Community will have is likely to be uniformly directed towards easing that path to a united Ireland.

First of all, at the psychological level, the more involved Irish people, North and South, become in a wider community, the less significant will appear their internal differences. At the level of the individual, contact with foreigners always tends to accentuate a sense of national identity. An Irishman never feels more Irish than when in an alien environment; his sense of sharing a common culture with his compatriots is then enhanced by the strangeness and alien quality of his current ambiance. And this is true on an all-Ireland basis; it is a matter of common experience that a Northern Protestant and a Southern Catholic finding themselves together outside Ireland readily make common cause, conscious of their common Irish-ness.

That which is true at the individual level is likely also to be true, at least to some degree, at the level of the political unit. Within a vast European Community the two parts of Ireland, sharing common interests in relation to such matters as agriculture and regional policy, must tend to draw together—and the fact that on some of these major issues the North and the Republic will have a common interest, divergent from that of highly-developed Britain, cannot be without significance in these conditions.

In this connection it is relevant to contrast the relationship between the interests of Northern Ireland and those of the independent Irish State as it was fifty years ago, when the country was first divided, and as it will be in the decades ahead, within the EEC.

As was pointed out in Chapter 1 the economic interests of the North's leading industries in 1920 seemed to require the maintenance of the link with Britain; the shipbuilding industry felt that secession from the United Kingdom would threaten the security of its principal market, in Britain, especially in so far as the construction of warships was concerned, while the linen industry (and other export industries in the north-east) felt that participation in an independent Irish State that might raise tariff barriers against goods from outside Ireland with a view to building up new industries in the rest of the country, could, by inducing retaliatory action by countries with which Ireland traded, endanger their markets in these countries. The rest of Ireland, by contrast, believed that it would benefit from securing the power to impose protective tariffs and quotas on imported goods.

This economic rationale for Partition will not exist within the EEC. Protected Irish industry has reached the stage at which it is prepared, both within the terms of the Anglo-Irish Free Trade Area Agreement and in the context of the EEC, to face free trade within the Community, and the inherently temporary divergence of interest between the north-east and the rest of Ireland on this issue has thus ceased to exist. As for shipbuilding, its importance in the economy of Northern Ireland has been drastically reduced, and its survival and prosperity in the years and decades ahead will be determined by considerations much broader than the political link with Britain.

What of the new considerations favouring a link between Britain and Northern Ireland that arose in the years after 1920? These are also likely to lose their importance under EEC conditions. Thus much of the agricultural benefits of participation in the UK will disappear quite quickly. The right of unrestricted access for all agricultural products to the British market, enjoyed by Northern Ireland as an integral part of the United Kingdom, but not hitherto by the Republic, will within the EEC be automatically extended to the whole of Ireland, which will indeed enjoy free access to the whole of the vast EEC market of 260 million people.

Secondly, the benefit of higher selling prices for farm products enjoyed by Northern Ireland will also, through the Common Agricultural Policy, be extended to the whole of Ireland. For example, whereas in 1969/70 the average price secured from the sale of milk products yielded just under 7p a gallon in the Republic, in Northern Ireland it produced just over 11p a gallon. No such difference will exist within the EEC.

Thirdly, the burden of subsidy required to supplement farm incomes accruing from the sale of farm products at market prices will be equalised. Within the EEC these price subsidies will be paid for out of the Common Agricultural Fund, to which member countries will contribute in proportion to their imports, especially of foodstuffs, and perhaps also, through a share of Value Added Tax, in proportion to their wealth. Thus whereas in 1969/70, in a necessarily inadequate effort to raise the average price received by farmers for milk to a remunerative level, the Irish taxpayer had to find subsidies amounting to over 4p a gallon for milk, considerably more than the UK subsidy of 2.5p per gallon, within the EEC the Republic's contribution to the Agricultural Fund from which these price subsidies are paid will be considerably *lower* per capita than the UK contribution, because Ireland imports much less foodstuffs per head than the UK, and has a lower per capita income.

Finally, whereas prior to EEC membership all the agricultural price subsidies in Northern Ireland, amounting to £15.8 m. in relation to a gross agricultural output of £148.2 m. in 1969/70, were paid from the UK Exchequer, thus providing a significant net transfer from Great Britain to Northern Ireland, within the EEC this benefit of participation in the UK, not secured by the Republic to any significant degree, will disappear, as the farm subsidies for both parts of Ireland will come from Community funds.

It is, of course, true that other agricultural subsidies, e.g. many of the production grants, will continue to be the responsibility of national governments under EEC conditions, thus maintaining a measure of transfers from the UK to Northern Ireland which will not accrue to the Republic, but the amounts involved represent only about half of the total farm subsidies payable by the UK to Northern Ireland prior to EEC membership.

Thus EEC membership will largely end the advantage secured by Northern Ireland farmers as a result of being within the United Kingdom, and will accordingly go far towards eliminating this particular economic obstacle to reunification, although the economy of Northern Ireland as a whole will continue to benefit to some degree from securing from UK funds certain production grants which in the case of the Republic have to be found from domestic taxation.

The other important economic consideration favouring the link between the UK and Northern Ireland is, of course, the arrangement under which a very substantial sum (in the region of £70 m.), is paid to Northern Ireland by the UK Government to subsidise the Province's social services. At its present stage of development the EEC is not organised in such a way as to affect this situation. There is no common social fund, similar to the Common Agricultural Fund; what is called the 'Social Fund' has a limited role relating only to problems of redundancy and retraining. Nor is there at present any proposal to create a common fund to finance the social security provisions of the Community, or to equalise them.

The absence of such an arrangement is, however, a source of considerable dissatisfaction to the trade unions of the Community, and must be seen as a serious gap in the Community system. It is not easy to see the logic of an arrangement under which there is free movement of the factors of production, and particularly of labour, as well as common financing of the subsidisation of agricultural exports, and of structural reform in agriculture, of redundancy payments and of resettlement and retraining of workers, and of regional developments, but not of social security.

As the Community moves towards economic and monetary union, and towards a more comprehensive approach to regional policy, it is almost inconceivable that it will not also develop a common social policy. The acceptance by the Community of the obligation to provide a common social security code, and to finance it on a Community basis, just as the Common Agricultural Policy is financed, appears inevitable in the long run, and as and when that happens, the economic advantage to Northern Ireland of participation in the UK social security system will disappear.

The potential effects of membership of the EEC on North-South relations do not stop there. The key issue in the question of national reunification is the transfer of 'sovereignty' from Westminster to an Irish Federal Government rather than any necessary transfer of powers from Belfast to Dublin. When the reform programme in Northern Ireland has been fully implemented, and when its government has been transformed from one involving a permanent monopoly of power by the majority in the North to one involving the joint participation of both communities, there may be little reason to transfer powers from the Government in Belfast to what will then become the Irish Federal Government.

But this question of the transfer of power from Westminster to an Irish Federal Government will lose some at least of its emotional impact if, as will happen within a developing EEC, much of the power normally exercised by Westminster in respect of Northern Ireland passes to Brussels. The system of devolution that has existed in Northern Ireland has reserved only a limited number of admittedly important functions to Westminster, the residual function of government being devolved to Stormont, subject, of course, to the power of the sovereign Westminster Government to revoke or modify this system of devolution at will. It is worth examining in greater detail the powers reserved to Westminster by the Government of Ireland Act. 1920.

These reserved powers may be summarised under the following headings:

> The Crown
> Foreign Affairs
> External Defence
> Nationality
> Post Office

Taxation of Profits and Incomes
Customs and Excise Duties
External Trade
Currency
Trade marks, patents, copyright
Miscellaneous (e.g. lighthouses, radio and transport).

A number of these matters are in law or in practice transferred to the Community institutions as a result of the United
Kingdom's decision to adhere to the Rome Treaty. This is true,
for example, of customs duties. Trade marks and patents are
matters to be covered by the proposed Convention for a Community Patent. External trade is, in principle, a Community
function under the provisions relating to the Common Commercial Policy of the EEC, although the implementation of
these provisions was postponed at the end of the transitional
period. The development of a common economic and monetary
policy would also bring currency matters within the ambit of
the Community. And if, as is far from certain of course, the
Community evolves into a political union as its founders intended, foreign policy and defence would also become Community matters. Finally, although the question of nationality is
not affected by the Rome Treaty, some of the privileges of
nationality—e.g. the right to enter another Community country to take up employment, or to move around within that
country—are controlled on a Community basis.

Thus the evolution of the Community in the years ahead
may well create a situation in which the actual powers exercised by Westminster as against those exercised by a reformed
regional administration could become very limited indeed. To
the extent that this happens, the question of whether these
powers are exercised by the government of the United Kingdom
or by the government of a federal Irish State would certainly
become less important in practical terms, and could also become less emotive for Northern Protestants.

Mention was made earlier of the possibility that within the
enlarged EEC the interests of Northern Ireland and the
Republic might well coincide on a number of issues, while
those of Great Britain might diverge from the general Irish
interest. This could be the case in particular with agriculture.
Although it is true that the pattern of agriculture in Northern
Ireland is rather different from that of the Republic, with much
more emphasis on intensive production of pigs and eggs,

requiring inputs of feeding stuffs, this divergence in patterns of production is likely to be reduced as a result of the application of the EEC Common Agricultural Policy; farming in Northern Ireland is likely to become more concentrated on milk and beef, as in the Republic. Such a closer alignment of agriculture in the two parts of Ireland would tend to bring them closer together also in terms of attitudes to agricultural policy within the Community.

The two parts of Ireland will in these circumstances have a common interest in the levels, both absolute and relative, of farm prices, and in arrangements for the subsidisation of export surpluses. Because of similarities of farm structures in the two areas, they will also have a common interest in Community farm structure policies. On all these issues their interests will tend to diverge significantly from those of Great Britain.

Again, with regard to regional policy, the two parts of Ireland have a common interest. It is true that Great Britain also has a domestic interest in the evolution of EEC regional policy because of its own regional problems in Wales and Scotland, and to a lesser extent Northern Ireland, but the importance of regional policy to Britain will be significantly less than its importance to both parts of Ireland. Moreover, a special dimension of EEC regional policy will apply in Ireland, which of its nature cannot arise in Great Britain—viz. the role of the Community institutions in assisting with the regional problems of frontier areas, where the existence of political boundaries has distorted or inhibited the economic development of the areas in question. Already the Community has interested itself quite deeply in this question, notably in relation to the complex frontier area where Germany, the Netherlands and Belgium meet, and where plans to develop this divided region are being organised under Community inspiration and leadership.

The Irish analogy is obvious; even before the terms of accession by the United Kingdom and Ireland were negotiated, Community officials had shown an interest in contributing to the solution of the problems of the Irish frontier regions whose economy was seriously disrupted by partition; notably the Derry/Donegal region, and also the Fermanagh/Cavan/Leitrim region.

The common interest of both parts of Ireland in Community agricultural and regional policies, which may contrast on a number of points with Great Britain's interests, is likely to bring North and South closer together, and to encourage co-operation between them within the Community, and in some respects also to create a divergence of interest between Northern Ireland and Britain. This possibility has long been recognised in some farming circles in Northern Ireland, quite independently of any political considerations.

This could create an interesting situation within the institutional structure of the Community. This structure is strongly biassed in favour of small States, and against larger ones. Thus the Republic of Ireland's representation in the European Parliament, on the basis of the existing indirectly elected European parliamentary institution, has been fixed at 10 seats out of 208, or almost 5%, for a country with barely 1% of the Community's population and about $\frac{2}{3}$% of its GNP. This scale of representation, almost five times that justified on a population basis, contrasts markedly with that of the United Kingdom which, with 22% of the Community's population will have only $17\frac{1}{2}$% of its voting power. As a result, the UK, although having a population 19 times that of the Republic will have a representation in the European Parliament barely three times that of its small neighbour!

This has significant implications for Northern Ireland, for unless the British Government, already squeezed in this matter of representation by the Community's bias in favour of smaller countries, decides to reduce still further Great Britain's fraction of the voting power in Parliament by allotting to Northern Ireland a disproportionate share of the UK representation, Northern Ireland cannot hope to have more than one member in the European Parliament, that being its share in relation to the population of the United Kingdom as a whole, viz. $2\frac{3}{4}$% of 36 seats.

That Northern Ireland, with over half as many people as the Republic, and a volume of domestic output and personal income over two-thirds that of the Republic, should have only one-tenth of the Republic's representation in the European Parliament is a somewhat disconcerting by-product of the province's role as a region of the UK on the one hand, and the Community's bias in favour of small States on the other.

Nor is this question of unequal representation confined to the European Parliament. Indeed the problem for Northern Ireland is even more serious in the other institutions, where it will have no independent representation. It is perhaps unlikely that either of the UK's two Commissioners, or its judge in the European Court of Justice, will be drawn from Northern Ireland, and although it is true that in the decision-making process of the Council of Ministers—if and when it votes by qualified or simple majority—the UK will have ten votes, these ministerial votes are cast as a unit by the representative of the country in question attending the particular meeting of the Council of Ministers. It is clearly unlikely that in the event of a conflict of interest on an issue between Northern Ireland and Great Britain—such as is quite likely to arise when agricultural matters, for example, are under discussion—these ten votes will bo cast by the UK Minister in favour of Northern Ireland's position and against the interests of the other $97\frac{1}{4}\%$ of the UK!

Thus the very fact that the institutional structure of the Community is heavily biassed in favour of smaller States (so that the Republic of Ireland with 1.1% of the Community's population will have almost 5% of the voting power in the European Parliament and at meetings of the Council of Ministers, while the Irish Commissioner will exercise 7% of the voting power in that body), operates against the interests of a region of a large State, whose interests within the Community will in any event tend to be submerged in those of the State to which it forms a part.

In these circumstances the interests of Northern Ireland will on a number of important issues be much better represented by the Republic of Ireland than by the UK, and the common interests of the two parts of Ireland, together with the fact that the Irish representatives in the Community will in practice be voicing the views of Northern Ireland and advancing its cause in such matters, when the UK representatives are pursuing an opposite course, must tend to bring the two parts of Ireland closer together. It is not totally inconceivable, indeed, that the Republic could make available to Northern Ireland part of its parliamentary representation, with a view to ensuring a more balanced overall Irish presence in the European Parliament, or could undertake to represent the interests of Northern Ireland in the institutions of the Community where these were not being furthered by the UK representatives—although for this to be politically acceptable in Northern Ireland would require a radical improvement in current North/South relations!

In the longer run this whole question of representation within the Community institutions could contribute to a reconsideration of Northern Ireland's relationship with the Republic. If over a period of time the identity of interest between the two parts of Ireland on vital issues within the Community became evident, and the divergence of interest between Britain and both parts of Ireland became equally clear, then this, together with the sense of frustration which Northerners could come to feel at having their interests misrepresented, so to speak, by the UK, could encourage the North to contemplate what would then be a more logical and valid arrangement—viz. the representation of Irish interests within the Community by ministers and parliamentarians of a united Ireland.

At the outset of this discussion of the relevance of membership of the EEC to the Irish problem it was remarked that it would be quite wrong in this context to look to the EEC as a panacea. The problem of Irish unity can be resolved only by Irishmen and women in Ireland, grappling with the real issues of living together in this small island. But enough has been said, perhaps, to suggest that in so far as membership of the European Communities by Ireland and Britain has relevance to the Irish question, it is likely to prove helpful to the cause of a peaceful reunion of the Irish people, rather than otherwise. The importance of EEC membership for Irish reunification is impossible to assess at this stage; it is not possible to see clearly any great distance ahead at a time when passion and violence dominate the Irish scene. But if some kind of normality is restored, and if the two parts of Ireland find themselves once again living in peace, internally and with each other, then the participation of both in the European Communities may well prove, for the reasons just mentioned, of greater importance to eventual reunification than anyone can imagine in 1972.

7. A Shared Heritage

In Chapters 2 and 3 the differences between North and South were explored—differences that grew deeper after the bulk of Ireland secured independence and went its own way. In Chapter 4 the extent of the current economic differences between the two parts of Ireland were examined in greater detail and in Chapter 5 the religious issue, which is fundamental to this division was considered. Then looking forward to the possibilities for Irish reunification in the future, the preceding chapter considered a number of factors working in favour of reunification, especially the impact of EEC membership. Before trying to draw the threads together with a view to seeing how we might bridge the differences, taking advantage of the factors mentioned in the last chapter, it is now time to take stock of what, despite everything, the Irish people, North and South share in common.

Above all the Irish people share their common history, their sense—sometimes distorted—of the importance of religion in the life of man, and their common economic and social problems. These have combined to give a distinct identity to the Irish people in the eyes of the world. However different Northern Protestants and Southern Catholics may feel themselves to be, what is most striking to anyone outside Ireland is how much they have in common. Whatever torturing doubts about the strength of Irish national identity may be felt by nostalgic Gaelic-orientated patriots in the Republic, and however much some Ulster Orangemen may declare themselves to have no share whatever in an Irish national identity, the separate identity of the Irish is not questioned outside Ireland. The characteristics of this identity as seen from outside, and above all as seen through British or American eyes, may not always be flattering to the ego of the Irish, but that is another matter. The popular image of most countries outside their own borders never measures up to the natives' vision of themselves—Ireland is not alone in that! What is relevant here is that to people outside Ireland the suggestion that there is no such thing as Irishness, or that Ulstermen in Northern Ireland are not Irish but British, evokes incredulity rather than acceptance.

Of course Irish history is seen from very different angles, through differently distorted lenses, in the two parts of Ireland —or perhaps one should say amongst the two communities, Protestant and Catholic. But what is important ultimately is not necessarily the different viewpoints from which this history is seen, but rather the fact that the two communities are looking at the same events, which are culturally important to both of them—and to no one else! A Southern Catholic knows what a Northern Protestant is talking about when he extols the merits of the defenders of Derry; he can appreciate the significance and importance of this event, although he sees this significance in different terms. But to an Englishman the preoccupation of Irishmen, Protestant and Catholic, with such remote events in their history, appears merely as an eccentricity—amiable, perhaps, prior to 1968, and sinister since then.

The significance of the cultural gap between the Irish as a whole and the British has begun to become clear to Northern Protestants only very recently. One of the most traumatic effects on Protestants in the North of the violent events since 1968 has been the growing realisation that Northern Protestant 'loyalty' to Britain was reciprocated only by blank incomprehension on the part of the British people. The failure of the British to see events in Northern Ireland from the Northern Protestant viewpoint shattered the confidence of many Northern Protestants. That the Northern Catholics, or the population of the Republic, rejected their viewpoint was irritating but in no way surprising or necessarily even disturbing; that the British failed to understand even why their viewpoint mattered was quite devastating.

The effects of this re-assessment have been most evident in the extreme Protestant leaders, Boal and Paisley. Just what illusions they may have had about Britain before the recent violence it is hard to say; if they had doubts, they kept them to themselves. But by the end of 1971 they no longer hid their disillusionment with Britain, and showed signs, most clearly of course in private discussion, but also, at least in Mr. Paisley's case, in what under public questioning he did *not* say, of being prepared in certain circumstances to re-consider their attitudes to Irish reunification. These very Irish figures, comprehensible to their fellow-Irishmen in a way in which they could never be comprehensible to a British audience, seemed to be bringing themselves to the point of recognising that they share more with their fellow-Irishmen, across the barricades of Belfast, than they have in common with the inhabitants of post-Christian Britain. The significance of this should not, of course, be exaggerated; few of their supporters would at this stage follow them far along this line, preferring to see the issues in traditional terms. The significance of this development is long-term rather than short-term. Nevertheless it cannot be ignored.

The cultural gap between the Protestant people of Northern Ireland and the British extends of course to the fruits of history as well as to history itself: to the kind of cultural ambiance that history has created in Ireland, North and South. The practical divisions between the two communities in Northern Ireland are in very many respects divisions peculiar to Irish society rather than divisions between a British system, shared by Northern Protestants, and an Irish system. The whole Orange versus Green concept is Irish; apart from a limited survival in Canada and in Glasgow the Orange institution at this stage in its history is an exclusively Irish phenomenon, rather than a manifestation of British culture in Ireland. The dominant role of religion in social life is no longer a feature of British society. Northern Protestant attitudes to sexual morality are more akin to Irish Catholic attitudes than to current British attitudes. The Northern educational system, although it has taken a somewhat different road from that of the Republic, is Irish rather than British in the extent to which it is divided along religious lines.

At a quite different level, traditional music, manners of speech, tastes in food, mental attitudes in Northern Ireland to the world outside Ireland—very many of the little things that go to make up the culture of everyday life—are closer to those of the rest of Ireland than to those of Britain, with some exceptions in relation to Scotland, with which the Ulster Scots culture (indeed the whole Irish culture) retains a number of links.

There are certain areas, however, where the division between the two communities is in some measure a British/ Irish phenomenon. One is sport, where Gaelic games are followed only by the Catholic community. Yet even here the division is not a clear-cut one, for in football the devotion of many Northern Protestants to soccer and especially to British soccer as a spectator sport is shared by quite a proportion of their Catholic neighbours especially in urban Belfast, and by a growing proportion of the population of the Republic. Moreover Protestants North and South, and a considerable section of Southern Catholics, especially urban middle-class Catholics, share a common interest in Rugby Football, which, like the Gaelic games of football and hurling, is organised on an all-Ireland basis.

Again, the trade union movement shows a certain Irish/ British polarisation—Catholic workers in the North tending to be members of Irish trade unions, and Protestant workers tending to be members of British trade unions. Here also the position is more complex than appears on the surface, however, for the structure of Irish trade unions is such that in the North many Catholics have to be members of British trade unions and some Protestants have to be members of Irish trade unions. Moreover even in the Republic a significant proportion of workers are members of British unions. And in any event all unions in Ireland, whether British or Irish, are affiliated to the Irish Congress of Trade Unions, whose headquarters are in Dublin, and which has a Northern Ireland Committee.

The fact that some of the main sporting organisations and the trade unions have maintained an all-Ireland structure, and that the Churches, Protestant as well as Catholic, have remained organised on an all-Ireland basis, testifies to the underlying sense of one-ness that has survived fifty years of Partition, even on the Protestant side. The idea of a re-alignment of church organisation involving a secession of the Northern Ireland parts of the Protestant churches and their incorporation within British church organisations, would be regarded by most Protestants, in the North as well as in the Republic, as quite ludicrous, and has never in fact even been suggested. The Irish-ness of the Protestant Churches in Northern Ireland is unquestioned, even by their most anti-Republican members.

When one turns to the question of national character, it becomes more difficult and more dangerous to generalise or to make firm statements. First of all, within any country regional divergences in attitudes and outlook often tend to loom larger in the minds of the inhabitants than the more elusive common heritage. Moreover the whole question is fraught with all the dangers of subjective judgments. At the same time outside observers are fairly unanimous in remarking on the greater importance of personal relations in Ireland than in other, larger, more anonymous countries, such as Britain. The sense of being part of a community is stronger amongst Irish people than amongst the British, and personal relations loom much larger in the forming of attitudes to public issues. At times the intrusion of personal considerations into public affairs can be damaging and dangerous; it has led to a survival of jobbery on a scale not paralleled in Britain—except at the top level in that country where the 'old boy' network still seems to operate! It also inhibits the achievement of efficiency, because of the fear of hurting the feelings, or hitting the pockets, of incompetent people in authority whose removal may be necessary to achieve better results.

At the same time life is warmer and more humane where personal considerations play a large part, as in Ireland, and a good deal of the difference in quality of life between Ireland and Britain derives from this. And though there are some differences between North and South in the way this more personal quality of life shows itself—in Ireland as in many other European countries the Northern temperament is less effusive and volatile than that of the Southerner—most outside observers would take the view that the differences between the Irish and English temperament is much greater than any internal differences between the temperaments of Irishmen in different regions of the country.

The Irish people North and South also have common problems, an element that can be a unifying force. In both areas there is the problem of the labour surplus, due to the large outflow from declining sectors of the economy, the relatively high birth rate and consequent rate of natural increase of population, and the unspectacular growth rate of the economy. This leads to high unemployment and emigration. Moreover within each of these two parts of Ireland there are internal regional problems—the Western region of each part having a much higher level of labour surplus, and in frontier regions these regional problems become cross-border problems, soluble only by development programmes organised jointly, in disregard of the boundary.

The problem of the declining sectors of the economy reflects the slow adaptation of the whole Irish economy to modern conditions. True, there are differences, in that in Northern Ireland the problem is rather one of adjusting an out-dated industrial structure, whereas in the Republic the main problem is the change-over from employment in agriculture to employment in industry and services. But both types of adaptation pose similar psychological problems for those affected, and the kind of economic development required to provide alternative employment is similar in both cases.

Moreover in other sectors the process of updating the economic structure takes the same form in both areas; for example the stresses and strains caused by the substitution of supermarkets and self-service stores for a system of retail distribution through traditional-type small shops are much the same North and South, and in both areas are perhaps more acute than in Britain, whose retail structure has been less antiquated.

The need for accelerated economic development has highlighted the role of the State and in a country which, both North and South, has been conservative in its attitudes, this can raise some fresh strains. These strains are perhaps more acute in Northern Ireland where an overflow from the British ideological debate of the post-war years, and the association of the Unionist Party with the Conservative Party in Britain, have made many Protestants very chary of State activity.

More rapid economic development also involves more foreign investment. While this fact is widely recognised, and while some of the traditional Irish xenophobia is suspended because of this recognition, the growing importance of foreign investment in Irish industry, and doubts in both areas as to the permanence and degree of commitment of some of these new firms to the local economy pose similar problems.

Both North and South are also suffering from some psychological strain as a result of the speed with which both areas have found themselves exposed to external influences. In the Republic these strains are evident in a vocal sense of uncertainty about the preservation of Irish cultural identity in the face of external cultural pressures; in Northern Ireland the majority has had to face the unpalatable fact that to the rest of the world their closed society, with its dominance by one religious group over another, appears an unlikeable anachronism, left over from the seventeenth century. And the Northern minority in turn has found it very difficult to adjust to the new situation in which it has found itself since the events of 1968–1969.

Both societies have also had to face the same kind of radical changes that have affected the rest of the world in recent decades; changes in family relationships, in attitudes of youth, in willingness to accept authority. While in some ways the effects of these changes have been muted in Ireland, the way in which they have affected Irish society is rather similar, North and South, and distinctly different from the way that British society has been affected. The changes in attitudes amongst young people have been less radical in Ireland than elsewhere, but the much more traditional character of Irish Society has ensured that the impact of these changes has been quite dramatic.

In both parts of Ireland the problem of the alienation of the urban working-class from society has to be faced. In the North inter-community strife has given this alienation a special form and a special outlet, for which there are no Southern equivalents. But the basic phenomenon is the same on both sides of the Border, and differs somewhat from that in Britain.

Irish cities are not impersonal anonymous concrete jungles. They are, in social terms, groups of villages, tightly interconnected geographically, but within each of which neighbours are almost as intimate with each other as in a rural village. The old Georgian tenements, and the newer city centre flats with their balconies and internal court-yards, and the straggling outlying working-class suburbs of Dublin, are none of them well suited to human needs, but they provide living conditions that give an outlet to the gregariousness of the urban working-class. The same is true of the little brick houses of working-class Belfast, and of its suburbs, on the lower slopes of Cave Hill and Black Mountain. Anonymous high-rise flats, although they exist in both Belfast and in Dublin as blunders of middle-class privacy-orientated planners, represent only a tiny minority of total working-class housing in these two cities.

As a result, however, deplorable the conditions thus created, and however disastrous the absence of adequate amenities for young people, city life in Ireland has not killed the personal, human element that is so important in Irish society. This has

meant that the Irish working-class reaction to cultural depriva-
tion through deficiencies in the educational system, and to a
class gap which few have proved able to surmount,[1] has been
different from the reaction of similar groups in British society.
The close inter-personal relations within such working-class
communities, and in many instances also the consolations of
religion, have helped to mitigate the sense of alienation of this
social group. In human terms this has made life more tolerable;
it has also, together with the emigration of some of those most
frustrated, reduced the pressure from this group for a radical
change in the social system, thus increasing the responsibilities
of the middle class to lead a movement for such a change.

Enough has, perhaps, been said to indicate that the problems,
economic and social, of North and South have more in common
than the problems of Northern Ireland have with those of
Britain. Hopefully, they might, therefore, be more readily solved
if they were tackled together by the peoples of the two parts of
Ireland. Certainly many of the problems of Northern Ireland
are more likely to be understood and approached intelligently
by an Irish Government, in whose considerations they would
necessarily loom large, than by a British Government which
must concern itself mainly with the rather different problems of
the 97% of the UK population living on the island of Great
Britain.

[1] See Economic and Social Research Institute Paper No. 48, *Social Status
and Inter-generational Social Mobility in Dublin*, by D. B. Hutchinson.

8. Towards a New Regime in the North

ONE of the features of the Civil Rights Movement that distinguished it from any earlier anti-Unionist organisation in Northern Ireland was the priority it gave to internal reform in Northern Ireland. The reunification of Ireland was seen by the organisers of this movement as something that should be left on one side while this internal reform was being pursued by non-violent agitation. And some at least of the Civil Rights leaders saw the reunification of Ireland as something to be secured only with the consent of a majority in Northern Ireland. In this way for the first time an attempt was made to take the Partition issue out of politics in the North, so that all who believed in individual freedom, social justice, and the ending of discrimination on grounds of religion, might be enabled to come together in this cause, whatever their views about the relationship of Northern Ireland with Great Britain or with the Republic of Ireland.

This attempt was not wholly successful. First of all very few people who believed in the union of Northern Ireland with Great Britain were in fact attracted to support the Civil Rights Movement. The combination of inherited prejudice against the minority, suspicion of Republican influences, doubts about any type of agitation involving street demonstrations, and the basic conservatism of many Northern Protestants, prevented more than a handful of the majority in the North from associating themselves with the Movement.

Moreover it proved impossible to prevent the agitation thus begun from gradually becoming bogged down in the old sectarian quarrel. The reaction of the Unionist Government and its police force to the Civil Rights Movement, which was clearly demonstrated at Derry in October, 1968, and the attack on the Civil Rights march at Burntollet in the Spring of the following year, together with the counter-reaction of the minority to the repressive tactics of the police, created the confrontations of August, 1969, and thus led to the subsequent recrudescence of militant activity by the IRA, many of whose supporters, especially in Northern Ireland, were not prepared in these conditions to continue to follow the non-militant policy laid down by their leaders. At the end of 1969 and in early 1970 this group broke with the rest of the organisation, to form the Provisional IRA.

But although the Civil Rights Movement, through the bitterness of the reaction it provoked in Unionist circles, eventually sparked off the very kind of sectarian conflict which its organisers had hoped and planned to avoid, it nevertheless achieved acceptance in principle—and to a very large degree implementation in practice—of its reform demands by the UK Government. Moreover its contribution to political thought in Northern Ireland, in the form of an attempt to side-track the Partition issue while a normal society was being created in Northern Ireland, has not been totally fruitless. It is of course true that the confrontation between the British Army and the Catholic population in the ghetto areas of Belfast and Derry in particular, which developed during 1970 and became so acute in 1971, aroused the latent dissatisfaction of the minority with any solution that fell short of a United Ireland in which they would be free of majority control by the Northern Protestants. Especially after internment in August, 1971, the issue of reunification was pushed back into the foreground, whence it had been carefully shunted both by the Civil Rights Movement and later by the Social Democratic and Labour Party. Political reactions outside Northern Ireland, both in Britain and in the Republic were partly responsible for this.

The significance of the Civil Rights Movement's approach to Partition had never really been understood outside Northern Ireland. Both in Britain and in the Republic many politicians failed to grasp that the principal leaders of the Northern minority were willing to leave this issue on one side for an indefinite period, if only the grievances of that minority could be remedied and injustice and discrimination eliminated. In the Republic internal differences within the ruling Fianna Fail party encouraged a resumption of sloganeering on the subject of Partition. In Britain frustration and despair about finding any solution within Northern Ireland, and a growing desire to get shut of the Irish problem once and for all, led some British politicians—notably Harold Wilson—to raise the question of reunification in the aftermath of the 1971 internment debacle. And the fact that the question of reunification was once again being seriously discussed in Britain, helped to bring it back into the forefront of Irish politics.

Nevertheless the work of the Civil Rights Movement and of the Social Democratic and Labour Party in 'long-fingering' reunification has not been entirely without result. It is notable that even the IRA groups have not sought immediate reunification, but rather an internal reform within Northern Ireland to be followed by reunification over a period of time. This means that despite all that has happened the gap between Unionist and anti-Unionist attitudes has remained narrower than in the past and a gradual solution of the problem of reunion is now arguably more feasible than would otherwise have been the case.

The first stage of any solution must lie in a reform of the institutions of government within Northern Ireland. An obstacle to this has been the lack of preparedness of the minority for this challenge. It is difficult to avoid the impression that the Civil Rights Movement and the Northern Opposition politicians were taken aback by the suddenness with which their reform demands were conceded in principle in Autumn, 1969, and were largely implemented in practice thereafter. They would seem to have been unprepared for this, and not to have thought out the logical next stage of their campaign— proposals for a reconstitution of the Northern Ireland system of government designed to end the sense of alienation of the minority and to give them what the British Home Secretary, Mr. Maudling, subsequently described as 'an active, permanent and guaranteed role' in the administration of Northern Ireland.

For two reasons the need for a programme of this kind became very urgent once the reform programme was conceded. First, the reforms, even if they had been implemented in every detail, were bound to be followed by a period of disillusionment. From the point of view of the average Northern Catholic two of the most important reforms were those affecting discrimination in employment and in housing. But acceptance of the need to eliminate discrimination in these matters, and the institution of a new system that would achieve this result in all future public appointments and housing allocations, can affect the overall employment and housing situation only over a period of many decades. Unless all the Protestants who had got jobs or houses they should not have got during the preceding fifty years were to be ousted and replaced by Catholics (which no one had ever suggested should be done) no dramatic results could come overnight from these reforms. The emotional impact of an announcement that the reforms were conceded, followed by a sudden realisation that the effects of this would be felt only over a very long period, was bound to be disillusioning, and it would have been desirable to have been ready at that point to move on immediately to the logical second stage of the campaign—a demand for a reform of the structure of government in Northern Ireland.

A second reason why it was important to move rapidly to the second stage was the improbability that the British Army would be able to maintain its peace-keeping role indefinitely, especially as elements in the IRA were likely to be unwilling to tolerate a situation in which the British Army and the minority remained on good terms.

Unfortunately, although understandably, the Civil Rights Movement and the political opposition were not ready for this situation. The Northern Ireland opposition parties, lacking in funds and in research and secretarial services, and overwhelmed by the volume of constituency work facing their members and by other demands on them, found it very difficult indeed to develop coherent policies; in the case of the Social Democratic and Labour Party the problem was made all the more acute by the fact that the party had only just come into existence, and that its parliamentary members were people of diverse views, unaccustomed to working together on the preparation of considered policy documents.

One of the first signs that thought was being given by the Opposition to the re-structuring of the system of government in Northern Ireland was the submission of a document to the Crowther Commission by John Hume, MP, in February, 1970. The propositions he put forward were:

1. It should be stated in any Constitution of Northern Ireland that any citizen or group has a constitutional right to advocate constitutional change by peaceful means.

2. Proportional representation should be reintroduced as the electoral system for both Stormont and local government elections, so as to ensure the full representation of minority opinion—not only of traditional opposition opinion but also of those who believe in the link with Britain but who cannot accept the sectarian base of the Unionist Party. The introduction of PR would also remove the political advantage of housing segregation, which serves only to perpetuate community divisions and problems.

3. A periodic referendum on the question of Northern Ireland remaining an integral part of the United Kingdom should be introduced, thus effectively removing the constitutional question from party politics and allowing for the development of normal politics.

4. A Bill of Rights should be enshrined in the Constitution to ensure full human and civil rights for all citizens irrespective of the Government in power. (This latter proposal was spelt out in more detail, drawing on the European Convention on Human Rights, the European Social Charter, the Universal Declaration of Human Rights, the UN Covenant on Human Rights, the UN Covenant on Economic, Social and Cultural Rights, the UN Convention on Civil and Political Rights, and Human Rights clauses in the Constitution of the Republic.)

It may be noted that this proposal did not contain any reference to the question of participation in government by representatives of the minority as a matter of right. Although the proposal for a joint government in Northern Ireland, representing both majority and minority, had been made by Fine Gael, the principal opposition party in the Republic, in its policy statement on Northern Ireland, published in September, 1969, the antipathy felt by most members of the Northern Opposition to the regime in Northern Ireland was such that it was only over a period that the idea of transforming this regime by joining it came to be seriously considered. Towards the end of 1970 it was reported that it was being mooted in opposition circles, and in the Spring of 1971 it became a matter of public discussion.

In June, 1971, the Northern Government went a certain distance towards meeting the growing desire of the Opposition to share in the power of government as of right. It proposed a system of Committees, in which the Opposition would play a disproportionate role. There were to be three new Committees —covering Social Services, Environmental Services and Industrial Services—in addition to the Public Accounts Committee already in existence. These Committees would have not more than nine members each, broadly representative of party strengths in parliament. Their members would receive fees, and their Chairmen—at least two of the four of whom would be members of the Opposition—would receive salaries. These Committees would consider major proposals of policy, review the performance of executive functions by the Government and its agencies, and, where the House deemed it appropriate, consider certain legislation at the Committee stage.

This proposal was welcomed quite warmly by members of the Opposition, but subsequent events—the refusal by the Westminster Government to order an enquiry into the deaths of two young men shot in Derry, and a visit by the Prime Minister to a meeting of the Orange Order—soon afterwards changed the whole climate of minority opinion, and led to the withdrawal of the Opposition from Parliament. This in turn was followed by the introduction of internment and a polarisation of the two communities.

By the Autumn of 1971 it was clear that nothing short of full Opposition participation as of right in the government of Northern Ireland, preceded by the ending of internment, would satisfy the minority and provide a solution to the internal problems of Northern Ireland. This seemed to be recognised by the British Home Secretary Mr. Maudling when, speaking in the Northern Ireland debate in the House of Commons towards the end of September, 1971, he adverted to the suggestion of Opposition participation in government in Northern Ireland, and raised only two difficulties, neither of them insuperable, viz. that those participating would have to condemn violence, and that they would have to accept the principle that Irish reunification should be achieved only by consent of a majority in Northern Ireland.

Whether this concept of minority participation in government had ever been acceptable to some members of the Unionist Government under Brian Faulkner, as there is some reason to believe might have been the case a month or so earlier, it was no longer acceptable to it at the time when the Home Secretary publicly raised the question. Within a few days of the Home Secretary's Commons speech, Mr. Faulkner had taken three opportunities to denounce the idea of a joint government and to proclaim that he would not serve in a government that contained people who looked forward to a united Ireland, even if they were dedicated to work for this aim only by peaceful means.

These declarations contributed more to putting an end to Mr. Faulkner's Premiership and the Stormont system of government than to scotching the concept a joint government, which alone appears capable of eventually bringing the sundered people of Northern Ireland together again under a regime in which both communities could have confidence. The alienation of the minority from government in Northern Ireland is the most fundamental problem facing the province after these years of violence, and such alienation can be ended only by participation in the decision-making process at the highest level.

Of course the establishment of a joint government is only one of a number of steps that would have to be taken to create normal conditions in Northern Ireland. As a necessary preliminary to this, parliament would have to be elected by proportional representation as proposed to the Crowther Commission by John Hume in February, 1970. His proposal that the right of any citizen to advocate constitutional change peacefully should also be formally recognised is another necessary preliminary to participation in government by citizens who look forward to a change in Northern Ireland's relationship with the Republic.

Again, if a Northern Ireland Government with representatives of a wide range of political viewpoints, minority as well as majority, is to work, the question of Irish reunification would need to be taken out of party politics—which might perhaps be achieved by the British Government's acceptance, in its March, 1972, initiative, of John Hume's proposal to have this matter put to periodic plebiscites, assuming that no agreement is reached on a long-term timetable for reunification before this joint government is established. (This potential benefit of the plebiscite arrangement would of course be completely negatived if the 1949 Ireland Act provision for approval by the Northern Ireland Parliament were also retained—as appeared to be envisaged at the time of the March, 1972, initiative.) Finally a Bill of Rights is also needed, as proposed by John Hume, to ensure that the people of Northern Ireland, whether belonging to the minority or the majority, will feel secure in the enjoyment of their human rights under this new system of government.

It is worth considering some of these issues in greater detail, for too little has been written or spoken about how a new system of government in Northern Ireland might actually work.

First of all, there is the need to modify the electoral system. The case for a change to some form of proportional representation is not confined to the desirability of ensuring fully proportional representation in parliament for the minority in Northern Ireland, but this is of course an important consideration. Normally the Opposition, defined for this purpose as parties other than the Unionists and Democratic Unionists, have held about 12 or 13 of the 52 seats in the Northern Ireland Parliament. Yet the strength of opposition opinion in the country is much greater than that. In purely religious terms, the 1961 Census, the last to contain details of religious affiliations, showed that 35% of the population were then Roman Catholics, and that this proportion was rising very slowly; (it had increased by .5% in the preceding ten years). However, the fact that there is a much higher proportion of children in the Catholic population has as its corollary a smaller proportion of adults, and consequently of adult voters in Northern Ireland only 31% were Roman Catholics in 1961.

At the same time the Northern Ireland Labour party, which for the purpose of this calculation is being included with the Opposition, has always drawn much, indeed most, of its support from Protestants, so that the total Opposition vote is significantly higher than the 31% of Catholics in the adult population. A study of recent elections, adjusting these results to allow for the probable voting strengths of both Unionists and Opposition in constituencies which were not contested, suggests that the total strength of the Opposition vote, before the events of 1969 at least, may have been about 36–37%. With such a vote, the Opposition parties should have secured 18–20 of the existing 52 seats under a proportional representation system.

The idea of a larger Northern Ireland Parliament has, however, secured a considerable measure of acceptance, and in the October, 1971, Green Paper on 'The Future Development of the Parliament and Government of Northern Ireland'[1] an

[1] Cmd. 560, HMSO, Belfast.

increase of 20–30 members has been envisaged. A Parliament with 80 members has, in fact, been mentioned; in such a Parliament the Opposition, as defined, would be likely to have about 28–30 seats, if the voting pattern as between Government and Opposition were similar to that at elections before the recent violence.[2]

There is, of course, more than one system of proportional representation. That used in Northern Ireland in several elections in the 1920s, and in use throughout the history of the Republic, involves the single transferable vote with multi-member constituencies. Under this system the voters mark the candidates 1, 2, 3, etc., in the order of their choice, voting on party or personal lines as they decide, and for as many or as few of the candidates as they choose. A quota is determined by dividing the number of votes by the number of seats plus one, and adding one vote. This is the lowest figure which could *not* be attained by more candidates than those there are seats for. Anyone attaining this quota is elected, and if he has more votes than the quota, this surplus is distributed to other candidates in proportion to the numbers of them who are named as second preferences on the ballot papers. By then eliminating the lowest candidates, and distributing *their* votes to the candidates next named on these ballot papers, and passing on further surpluses wherever candidates get more than the quota, the election of the requisite number of candidates is completed, the final panel of elected candidates thus representing as accurately as possible the span of opinion in the constituency.

From the voter's point of view the system is not complex; he or she simply votes in order of choice. The complexity arises only in the counting of votes. Among the advantages of the system are the flexibility it offers to the voter, who is not confined by any party strait-jacket but can cross-vote at will. In this respect it differs significantly from the party list system, used in many Continental countries, under which the electors vote for parties rather than individuals, although it is possible to introduce into the party list system a measure of individual preferences amongst the candidates of the chosen party, or

[2] The emergence of the Alliance Party, the Democratic Unionist Party, and the Vanguard Movement has, of course, radically altered the political situation in Northern Ireland, invalidating any assessment based on past voting patterns. Indeed it invalidates the very concept of a Government Party and Opposition groups.

even, in some cases, amongst candidates other than those of the chosen party. The Northern Ireland Labour Party has indicated that it favours this list system, but the SDLP seems to prefer the more familiar alternative vote system.

It is incidentally worth noting that another advantage of the alternative vote system in the Northern Ireland situation is that it should tend to concentrate support on moderates. Thus the next preference of extremist voters will tend to go to more moderate candidates of the same community, so that if the extremist is eliminated his votes may help to elect a moderate. At the same time, some voters choosing moderate candidates of their own community, may prefer—at any rate when the polarisation of the communities becomes less extreme than at present—to pass their next preference votes to a moderate candidate of the *other* community, rather than to an extremist of their own community.

The election of an enlarged parliament by proportional representation would, however, be only a first step towards a solution that could bring the Northern minority within the area of consensus politics, ending its alienation and securing from it once again a measure of acceptance of the authority of government. In view of all that has happened in the years from 1968 onwards, and especially in the period after the introduction of internment in August, 1971, nothing short of a minority right to participation in a new kind of government of Northern Ireland for a prolonged period seems capable of securing this objective. Whether and to what extent such an arrangement would have to be accompamied by some kind of a defined prospect of reunification if it were to secure the acceptance of the minority is another matter—which will be considered in the next chapter.

Leaving that issue on one side and presuming for the moment the existence of a prospect of reunification that would be sufficient to secure the acceptance by the minority of a re-constituted government of Northern Ireland, while not alienating the majority in the North to the point where *their* consent to such a government would be withheld, a number of problems would nevertheless remain to be solved.

The principal obstacle raised in the way of such a joint government when this proposal was actively discussed in the period after the introduction of internment was the objection by the Northern Premier, Mr. Brian Faulkner, to the presence in a Northern Ireland Government of people who did not accept as indefeasible the constitutional link of Northern Ireland with Great Britain. This objection never seemed a tenable one, and by raising it at the end of September, 1971, immediately after the House of Commons Debate on Northern Ireland, Mr. Faulkner seemed to be gratuitously going out on a limb that—even if his rejection of the transfer of control over security in March, 1972, had not brought his regime to an end—would in time have proved fatal to his survival.

In that debate the British Home Secretary, Mr. Maudling, had discussed this question and had contented himself with raising two difficulties which gave the impression of being carefully selected because they could be easily overcome. These two points were that anyone serving in such a government should reject the use of violence and that they should also accept that reunification should come about only with the consent of a majority of the people of Northern Ireland. As these had been two principal planks in the platform of the Social Democratic and Labour Party since its foundation, Mr. Maudling's speech was very widely interpreted as giving the green light to the concept of a joint government.

Whether the Home Secretary (who must have had access to early drafts of the Northern Ireland Government's Green Paper on the Future Development of the Parliament and Government of Northern Ireland which was published a month later) was under the impression that such a proposal would be acceptable to the Northern Ireland Government or whether he spoke in these terms without knowing what their reaction would be, is not clear, but the statement and subsequent reiteration by the Northern Premier of his objections to this concept suggests that there had not been a meeting of minds between the two Governments on this subject.

Mr. Faulkner's objection was on grounds of the principle of cabinet responsibility, and must be seen in the context of the 1949 declaration by the UK Government in the Ireland Act of that year, that the reunification of Ireland could come about only with the consent of the Northern Ireland *Parliament*. This difficulty would, of course, be avoided if this question of reunification were either to be the subject of some prior agreed timetable, before the new governmental system was introduced, or, indeed, if it were to be left to a subsequent decision by the *people* as distinct from the *parliament* of Northern Ireland.

As has already been pointed out, the latter solution had in fact been proposed by John Hume in February, 1970, over eighteen months earlier. Of course, the fact that the technical objection by Mr. Faulkner on grounds of a need for cabinet responsibility for policies put to parliament could be side-stepped in this way does not necessarily mean that Mr. Faulkner and his colleagues would accept such a side-stepping; they could, for example, try to insist on the indefeasibility of the guarantee in the Ireland Act—although anyone trying this tack would very quickly find himself up against that slippery instrument, the British Constitution, which proclaims the power of parliament to do anything, including change its mind, and break its promises!

More practical and more serious objections to the joint government proposal could be raised on other grounds, however. Thus, for example, it could be suggested that even if the issue of reunification were satisfactorily dealt with the span of opinion which a joint government would have to bridge would be so wide that agreement on many other more immediate issues might be impossible to find; and that, indeed, such a government would be open to disruption by one extreme, or worse still, by both extremes together.

But while this objection has more substance, it still suffers from the defect of assuming a cabinet system of government *à l'anglaise* which is not, of course, the only possible system of government. In other countries, such as Switzerland, governments span virtually the whole political spectrum; although it must be said that this feature of the composition of the Swiss Federal Council is not a constitutional requirement, as it is proposed that it should be in Northern Ireland, but rather a matter of convention that has grown up over a period of over 120 years. In the early years after the present Swiss Constitution came into existence in 1848, single-party government was the norm; it was only gradually that it came to be accepted that more than one party should participate in government, and, later, that the Federal Council should, as far as practicable, reflect the composition of the parliament in terms of parties, cantons and languages—a difficult task with a body whose membership is only seven! Moreover, quite apart from the obvious difference between a convention emerging gradually over a period of decades and a solution imposed at a point in time on a deeply divided community, there may be sufficient differences between the Swiss and Irish temperaments to make the analogy a somewhat strained one!

Nevertheless although the fact that an analogous system *works* in Switzerland is no proof that it would work in Northern Ireland, the fact remains that there is nothing inherently impossible in the concept of a system of government by all, or most political groups. Such a system is alien to traditional British and Irish thought, save in so far as an *ad hoc* national government may be formed by common consent for the period of an emergency. But that does not mean that where no other system would be acceptable, because of the unwillingness of each of two political groups to live under a government in which it had no say, a joint government should not be tried; nor does it mean that it might not work—if for no other reason than because of a common realisation that no practicable alternative exists, other than direct rule from Britain or government by a Commission appointed by the British Government and not democratically elected. The knowledge that a particular solution is the only one that can give them a voice in government could concentrate the minds of politicians wonderfully!

Moreover although such a government could be subject to continual strains, and to sharp divergences on policy issues, the area in which such differences could exist and could exercise a divisive influence would be considerably circumscribed in a governmental structure where many of the key powers of government have always been exercised elsewhere—at Westminster, and in the future, in Brussels—and where others would be strictly limited by constitutional provisions guaranteeing a wide range of human rights from interference by the Government of Northern Ireland. If, in addition, control of security is vested in the Westminster Government, there might not be much room for really serious disagreement even between very diverse political groups.

Some indeed have wondered whether a body with such limited functions as those that a Northern Ireland Parliament might have in future if a Bill of Rights were introduced which it could not amend, and if control of security were transferred to Westminster, really needs an executive at all. After all, county councils seem to manage without executive committees comprising members of one party only and acting on the principle of collective responsibility. Given that Northern Ireland has a smaller population than the administrative area of the West Riding of Yorkshire exclusive of boroughs, and has barely twice the geographical area, some people have wondered why it has to have a system of government involving a parliament, executive and judiciary on the model of the United Kingdom itself. Some might even be so unkind as to suggest that Mr. Brian Faulkner's proposals for a system of parliamentary committees would, on the model of county councils, provide a sufficient super-structure of executive authority without bothering with having a Northern Ireland Government at all!

The analogy with a county council is certainly suggestive, even if not necessarily compelling. Given the outstanding failure of the system of government in existence in Northern Ireland for fifty years, it is certainly difficult to argue that there is such a vital need to keep it intact in precisely its present form that any suggested change must be ruled out forthwith. While the answer to the problem is probably not to turn the area into the equivalent of a county, with a system of government accepted as appropriate to a county, it is at least possible that something relevant to the governmental needs of Northern Ireland can be learnt by considering a whole range of possibilities lying between the system of government of a county and that of a sovereign State.

Thus whatever fears may legitimately exist about the practicability of getting the elected representatives of two deeply divided communities to work constructively together in an executive organ of government, or something broadly equivalent to such an organ, the possibility that such a system can be made to work, strongly reinforced by the near-certainty that nothing else can, must not be dismissed out of hand.

One danger, however, would be that any such scheme of government could be sabotaged by extreme elements refusing to work the system. What would happen, it may well be asked, if Vanguard supporters and Provisionals alike decided, while accepting election to parliament, to abstain from the assembly? How then could a government be formed on a basis proportionately representative of the parties? Alternatively would there not be a danger that in such a situation even some moderate elements in one community might feel constrained also to abstain from government?

This possibility must be faced. But the proportional representation system using the single transferable vote has hidden resources, possibly not suspected by those who have not had experience of its remarkable flexibility. It would be entirely possible to provide that if the members of any group or groups failed to take their place in parliament, or even if they did so but refused to participate in the supreme legislative function of choosing an executive, they would be disqualified, and the count of votes that had elected them would be resumed, eliminating them as if they had failed to secure enough votes for election, and passing their preferences on to the next preferred candidate of each voter.

Such a system would ensure that if extremists refused to play their part in the system, moderates would automatically, and retrospectively, so to speak, be elected in their places, drawing their authority from the electorate. Such an arrangement would on the one hand provide the strongest incentive to all concerned, extremists included, to participate in the system and would on the other hand strengthen moderate forces in parliament should extremists refuse to play their part. There is thus, perhaps, rather more chance than might appear at first sight that a system of joint government might be made to work in Northern Ireland, as part of a settlement of the intractable problem posed by this divided community. An essential part of such a system, however, would be a Bill of Rights that would assure all the members of both communities that they would be protected against exploitation, discrimination and repression. The content of such a Bill of Rights would be for negotiation. The reform programme as contained in the Downing Street Declaration of 20 August, 1969, and the Joint Communiques of 29 August and 10 October, 1969, should be involved in it—including those aspects of the reform programme which, as pointed out in the well-documented Commentary on the Northern Ireland Government's White Paper of 20 August, 1971, had not in fact been implemented up to that time.[3]

[3] This Commentary was published by the *Irish News* in September, 1971. Among the points made in it are that:
   a. The power of the Police Authority to retire police officers who misbehave had been circumscribed by Section 7 (2) of the Police Act (Northern Ireland), 1970.
   b. The independent tribunal to consider complaints against the police, provided for in Section 13 (2) of this Act, had not been established.
   c. The system of independent public prosecutors announced on October 10, 1969, had not been set up.

Other elements might be the European Convention on Human Rights, the Universal Declaration of Human Rights, the United Nations Covenant on Human Rights, the United Nations Covenant on Economic, Social and Cultural Rights and the United Nations Convention on Civil and Political Rights—all of them referred to in John Hume's evidence to the Crowther Commission in which he sought a Bill of Rights.

The method of guaranteeing such a Bill of Rights is a matter for discussion. Mr. Harold Wilson has proposed for this purpose a mixed Commission of members of the United Kingdom and Northern Ireland Parliaments. Other suggestions have included a blocking power for a reformed Northern Ireland Senate in which the minority would have control. One could also visualise a blocking vote by, say 25%, of the Northern Ireland House of Commons. But to many Irish people a system of judicial guarantees would be more attractive.

Because under the British Constitution Parliament is sovereign, there can be no judicial review of the constitutionally of parliamentary decisions in Great Britain. But such a review

---

d. The undertaking given by the Northern Ireland Government in November, 1968, to withdraw special powers that are in conflict with international obligations had not been implemented.

e. The Parliamentary Commissioner for Administration and the Commissioner for Complaints could investigate individual cases only and could not therefore take into account a broad pattern of discrimination —despite the fact that the Northern Ireland Government commentary on the Cameron Report had promised that the proposed Commissioner for Complaints system 'would cover maladministration (in the broad sense)'.

f. Two years after the commitment to require public bodies to adopt an approved code of employment procedure, the required code had not been adopted by half of the local authorities.

g. The promise in the Communiqué of October 10, 1969, that public authority contracts would require a declaration of an aim to have equality of employment opportunity without regard to political, as well as religious, considerations, had been dropped, and many public authorities have not yet required contractors to sign the undertaking with regard to religious discrimination.

h. Despite the promise that half of the members of the Community Relations Commission would be Catholics, and the statement in the White Paper of August 20, 1971, that this was the case, less than half the members were in fact Catholics.

i. Further action proposed in the Communiqué of October 10, 1969, against discrimination in private employment had not been forthcoming.

system exists not alone in the Republic of Ireland, where in a significant number of cases since the 1937 Constitution was adopted, laws passed by the Oireachtas have been found to be unconstitutional and thus null and void, but also in Northern Ireland, whose laws must be compatible with the Government of Ireland Act, 1920. That Act provides (Sections 50–53) for the determination by the Judicial Committee of the Privy Council and the House of Lords of questions arising with respect to the validity of laws passed by the Northern Ireland Parliament. Thus in both parts of Ireland the concept of judicial review of the validity of legislation alleged to be in conflict with constitutional guarantees is a familiar one. There is, perhaps, a good deal to be said for securing human rights by this means rather than by a political blocking mechanism whose employment could exacerbate political differences, and whose operation is unlikely to command general assent.

Of course the operation of such a judicial review system would require the constitution of an appropriate judicial tribunal, acceptable to the minority as well as to the majority. One method of achieving this might be to require the agreement of a two-thirds or three-quarters majority of parliament to the nomination of judges to this constitutional court, or perhaps (if, as is suggested below, the new system of government envisaged a Deputy Prime Minister to be chosen by whatever members of parliament did not vote for the Prime Minister, or by the later preferences of voters under an alternative vote system), a Deputy Premier could be given the nomination of, say, three of five judges, the other two to be chosen by the Prime Minister. No doubt, other formulae could also be suggested; there should in any event be no real difficulty about finding an acceptable way of constituting such a Court if the other problems in the way of a system of joint government within Northern Ireland could be overcome.

Before discussing further the possible function, and method of choice, of a Deputy Prime Minister, something should be said about the choice of the Prime Minister—assuming, of course, that such an executive office is retained, under this or some other title.

The Prime Minister could be elected by Parliament, or chosen by the members of a government themselves elected proportionately by parliament, or selected, subject to the approval of a majority in parliament, by the Governor or other British Representative.

The latter system might seem unlikely to be acceptable to the minority, but it could, perhaps, have some merits from their point of view. The Governor or other British Representative, in choosing a member of Parliament to put forward as Prime Minister might have regard to his acceptability to the minority, subject always to the consideration that he must be capable of securing the support of a majority in Parliament. In certain circumstances the person selected might not necessarily be the man whom the members of parliament representing the majority community would themselves have chosen if the initiative had been left to them—but he might nevertheless be able to command a majority in the House. In the confused and fragmented political scene of Northern Ireland in the years ahead, there could be something to be said for the system of selection of Prime Minister that is common in most parliamentary democracies—by a constitutional Head of State or his representative—rather than for leaving the matter completely to the initiative of the parties and parliament.

If the Prime Minister were either elected by Parliament on party initiatives, as is in fact the (rather unusual) constitutional position in the Republic of Ireland, or on the nomination of the Governor or British Representative, should he then have the task of choosing members of a government that will be proportionately representative of the various groups in the House, or should he have his government chosen for him by parliament, voting proportionately? The former method places a burden on the representative of one community greater, perhaps, than any likely degree of confidence in him on the part of the other community is likely to justify. This might, perhaps, be overcome, by first electing a Deputy Prime Minister, and then providing that the choice of the remainder of the government, to be proportionately representative of the different groups, be made by the Prime Minister and Deputy Prime Minister jointly. Some provision would have to be made for their failing to agree, however, and that could pose difficulties.

The advantage of such an arrangement would, however, be that more suitable personnel might emerge in this way than if the choice were left to a system of election of Ministers by Parliament, and that the team might prove more cohesive if it were selected in this way by the Prime Minister and Deputy Prime Minister. The prior choice of the government by parliament, followed by the election of a Prime Minister (and perhaps subsequently a Deputy Prime Minister) by the government thus elected, is, however, another alternative.

The merit of having a Deputy Prime Minister chosen in the manner suggested earlier—viz. by the votes of those who did not vote for the person chosen as Prime Minister, or by the later preferences of voters under an alternative vote system, would be that the minority would in effect find themselves with a leader in government, while at the same time an election along sectarian lines would have been avoided. The Deputy Prime Minister would symbolise in a personal way the right of those who did not give their confidence to the chosen leader of the majority to participate in government. He could act for the Prime Minister in his absence, thus making clear the reality of participation in government by the minority. He could also play a role in the allocation of portfolios within the government —a function which the minority would scarcely be prepared to leave solely in the hands of the leader of the majority—and, if the Prime Minister and himself were chosen first, and given the responsibility for *choosing* members of the government as well as allocating portfolios, he could participate in this selection process also. Some provision would in either case be necessary to deal with the problems that would arise should the two men fail to agree on either of these issues.

In suggesting these alternative approaches to the complex problem of establishing a system of joint government in Northern Ireland it is not intended to imply that this analysis is in any way exhaustive. There are no doubt other solutions. But at least the exercise may suggest that there are possible solutions to the problem, given sufficient goodwill on both sides to attempt the experiment.

At the other end of the time-scale, the proposals for joint government here outlined must themselves be viewed as something less than permanent; although clearly the minority would require a guarantee that this system would continue so long as the members of the minority felt it necessary. A system that eliminates all political opposition, by incorporating all groups of significance in government, does not seem likely, in the conditions of Britain and Ireland at any rate, to provide a satisfactory long-term solution. Any new constitutional pro- visions should therefore provide for a return to a normal parliamentary system if the consent of, say 75% of parliament or people is secured to such a proposal. Hopefully, over time the proposed system of joint government could lead to an end to the sectarian polarisation of Northern Ireland politics and to the emergence of some other division, possibly on the basis of divergent economic ideologies. In this event the people and politicians of Northern Ireland might feel themselves ready to return to a more normal type of parliamentary system, and this possibility should be faced and provided for.

But the immediate issue is not when and how Northern Ireland can hope to achieve a normal parliamentary system with alternating governments, but whether and under what conditions any solution of its internal problems can be found that will take account of the differences in its peopl's attitudes towards the issue of reunification. To what extent has this now been firmly re-introduced as a central issue into Northern Ireland politics, despite the earlier attempt of the Civil Rights Movement and the Social and Democratic Labour Party to long-finger it pending the achievement of internal reforms? And how can it best be tackled in a manner that might secure the consent or acquiescence on both communities? That is the question that must be examined in the concluding chapters of this book.

9. Towards Changes in the Republic

THROUGHOUT most of the past half-century the issue of Irish reunification was debated in somewhat simplistic terms. Because to both sides it appeared at first a temporary arrangement (although of course this was not publicly admitted by leaders of the majority in the North), relatively little thought was given to how it could be brought to an end, or even as to how the divergence between the two parts of Ireland could be prevented from widening. Northern Unionists were content with a 'no surrender' attitude, which some of them in their hearts did not take too seriously, and the Northern minority and the bulk of the people in the rest of the country were equally content to assert a claim to unity without pursuing very far the question of how this ambition might be realised. As the years passed the attitude of many supporters of Irish reunification imperceptibly and unconsciously changed from a presumption that Partition was temporary and would be brought to an early end, to an equally unconscious acceptance of it as an indefinitely continuing feature on the Irish landscape, but this underlying change of private attitudes brought no change in public policies. From time to time politicians in the Republic were moved to public statements of abhorrence of the political division of the island and at certain periods this sporadic competition in oratory developed into a campaign against Partition; most notably, perhaps, in the period 1948–1949, when Mr. De Valera took advantage of a spell in Opposition after sixteen years of government to launch a world-wide campaign on the subject. This campaign continued into the early 1950s, aided by a fund collected, rather tactlessly from the point of view of

Northern Unionist sentiment, at the gates of Catholic churches, and punctuated by the declaration of the Republic in 1949, and by the British guarantee in the consequential Ireland Act, 1949, of the Northern Ireland Parliament's right to decide the reunification issue.

The IRA border raid campaign of the years from 1956 onwards introduced a new element into the controversy, which, however, had no lasting effects, except on Northern Unionist attitudes. By the early 1960s the whole question seemed to be back where it had started, except that opinion had become accustomed to the fact of Partition, and pessimistic about prospects for its disappearance in the forseeable future.

Within Northern Ireland these decades saw many fluctuations in the attitude of the minority, ranging from abstentionism to limited participation in the governmental system, and even, at certain periods, an abdication by the constitutional Nationalist Party of its role in the face of Republican determination to contest seats at elections. (Fearing that to put forward candidates as it had done for decades previously would 'split the vote' and let the seats concerned go to the Unionists, the Nationalists temporarily ceded the ground to abstentionist Republicans, possibly believing that this threat to their political control of the minority would go away if left to blow itself out, as in fact eventually happened.)

The 1960s saw the emergence of a new attitude amongst the Northern minority, however. In the aftermath of the border raids and the temporary takeover of parliamentary representation by abstentionist Republicans, the mood of the minority switched back towards acceptance of a measure of involvement with the system; a willingness to try co-operation. One of the earliest protagonists of this policy was Mr. G. B. Newe, later, towards the end of 1971, to be appointed a member of the Northern Ireland Cabinet in a belated effort by Mr. Brian Faulkner to lend credibility to his government. But it received a measure of support as time went on from Nationalist politicians also, amongst them Mr. Paddy Gormley, MP, brother of Mr. Tom Gormley, who in early 1972, with two Unionist MPs, joined the Alliance Party.

It is against this background that one must see the analysis of minority attitudes in the Rose Survey, carried out in 1968 and briefly summarised in Chapter 5. This Survey was undertaken just at the end of this 'honeymoon' period, which had also been marked by the exchange of visits at Prime Minister level initiated by Mr. Sean Lemass in 1965.

But it is also against this background that one must see the emergence of the Civil Rights Movement. The tactical approach of this Movement reflected the shift in minority attitudes during the 1960s towards an attempt to work the system by concentrating on a political evolution within Northern Ireland as a preliminary to, and indeed a condition precedent of, any move towards seeking reunification by consent. Of course the Civil Rights Movement did not accept the rather formless drift towards co-operation that had marked the years before 1968; it adopted a positive policy of non-violent demonstration in pursuit of its aims, conscious, no doubt, of the strong possibility that such a show of independence and self-confidence by those who had suffered from the system of government in Northern Ireland since 1920 would be likely to arouse opposition and even physical resistance by supporters of the regime.

But although its tactics were aggressive rather than passive, its strategy was similar to that which had emerged more or less haphazardly amongst the minority during the immediately preceding years: tackle the internal problems of Northern Ireland in the first instance, and leave the issue of reunification on one side for the time being, to be settled later by agreement in the light of the new and, hopefully, saner situation that would emerge following the battle for reforms.

Despite the fact that the conservatism of most Northern Protestants, and their suspicion of Republican influences in the Civil Rights Movement, prevented that Movement from mobilising significant support from the Protestant community (although many Protestants did, of course, support the reforms when they were introduced), this development nevertheless changed the character of the Northern problem. Because the Civil Rights Movement was content to leave the Partition issue to be decided at a later stage, in a, hopefully, different atmosphere created by reforms, its reform programme was much more difficult to resist than any previous Opposition movement to the Northern Government. The Northern Government might convince a high proportion of its own supporters that the Civil Rights Movement was, despite its new policies, only anti-partitionism under another guise; it could not so easily persuade opinion outside Northern Ireland of this thesis. Moreover because civil rights had become a fashionable issue in other countries during the 1960s, and because the campaign—and any attempt to repress it—was transmitted with all the instantaneity and impact of television, the effect of the Civil Rights Movement on opinion outside Northern Ireland was greater than, perhaps, even its organisers had ever conceived possible. Had it been merely another stage in a long-drawn out campaign against Partition, it is doubtful whether, even with the aid of television, it could have had the same effect on opinion in Britain and elsewhere. The reaction to this campaign culminated in the violence of August, 1969, the intervention of the British Army to prevent a pogrom, and the granting of the reforms—subject to a certain amount of subsequent delay and whittling down, referred to earlier. In retrospect one is forced to wonder whether the Civil Rights Movement, and the politicians associated with it who later formed the Social Democratic and Labour Party, were prepared for the measure of success they achieved, and for the speed with which it was secured. The logical corollary of the anti-discrimination reform programme would have been a demand for a right on the part of the minority to participate in government, yet this demand was not made until much later, long after the minority in Belfast and Derry had come into conflict with the British Army.

The extent to which the new approach—concentrating on internal changes within Northern Ireland and leaving the Partition issue for later settlement—had taken deep root amongst the minority became evident during the period from August, 1969, until August, 1971, when internment was introduced. Throughout this period the Partition issue remained in the background, despite the increasing polarisation between Protestants and Catholics. It was only after the introduction of internment that the emphasis of minority attitudes began to switch back from internal change within the North to national reunification as an immediate aim. This reversal of emphasis in the autumn of 1971 was encouraged by the Wilson proposals, which envisaged an agreement on ultimate reunification, followed by a fifteen-year transitional period. It was given further impetus by the radio and newspaper interviews with Rev. Ian Paisley towards the end of 1971, when his proposals for constitutional change in the Republic, and deliberate side-stepping of questions about his attitude to reunification if these changes were effected, hinted at a possible change of attitude on this issue.

By the beginning of 1972 there was, moreover, evidence of similar stirrings in non-Paisleyite Northern Protestant opinion. The sense of insecurity of the Northern majority, and their fear that even if this crisis were overcome, the whole cycle of violence could start again in the future, seemed to be beginning to lead some more thoughtful members of the Protestant community to ask themselves whether there might not be something to be gained by examining the question of the kind of Ireland that might emerge if the two parts of the country were eventually to be reunited. Speeches by Richard Ferguson, a former Unionist MP, from December, 1971, onwards in which he addressed himself to the need to consider the possibility of a new non-sectarian united Ireland, underlined this new mood.

Thus, the failure to find a solution within the context of Northern Ireland based on the willingness of the minority in the late 1960s to leave the reunification issue on one side for the time being and to concentrate rather on internal reforms, had created by the start of 1972 a situation in which the whole question of a united Ireland had again become a live issue. Now, however, reunification seemed to have rather more prospect of realisation within a reasonable period than had seemed to exist at any time during the first forty years of the existence of Northern Ireland, when a sporadic campaign was being waged against Partition. Historians will, no doubt, debate the relative contributions to this new situation of a multiplicity of factors at work during the period from 1969 onwards, and especially in the closing months of 1971. These factors will probably include the following:

1. The policy vacuum on the side of the minority after the concession of the reform programme in August and October, 1969, which, in retrospect, can be seen to have inhibited change in the political structure of the North during this period.

2. The intransigence of the Unionist Government and Party when the proposals for minority participation in government in Northern Ireland emerged during the course of 1971.

3. The British Government's internment decision and that Government's failure, influenced, no doubt, by repeated Army promises of imminent victory over the IRA, to take any initiative in the closing months of 1971 to recover the ground thus lost.

4. The brutality associated with internment, and the failure of the British Army authorities to prevent some of its units from behaving in a manner that alienated the goodwill of even the most moderate members of the minority.

5. The disturbing effect on Northern Protestant opinion of the IRA campaign in the period after internment, and the growing belief amongst Protestants in Northern Ireland that the British Government, politicians and people neither understood their situation nor cared enough about it to sustain a prolonged campaign.

6. The reintroduction of the reunification issue into the sphere of practical politics by the Harold Wilson initiative of late 1971.

7. The emergence in the Republic of a movement favouring a more liberal and pluralist society, which for the first time offered Northern Protestants some hope that a united Ireland would not necessarily be simply an enlarged version of what they had always seen as a Republic dominated by Roman Catholic teaching and influence.

All of these factors, and perhaps others besides that may not be evident to an observer writing early in 1972, myopically close to the events in question, no doubt played their part, for nothing less than a complex combination of many causes could account for the emergence of a willingness on the part even of a thinking minority of Northern Protestants to start giving serious consideration to a solution involving eventual reunification in some form.

The ultimate significance of this shift in opinion is unknowable in early 1972; but enough has happened to make it worth considering seriously ways in which it might prove possible to overcome the obstacles to reunification that have been strengthened in the past half-century, reinforcing the basic inter-community hostility that initially led to Partition. The shape of an eventual solution, rather than the practical path towards its negotiation, will be the theme of the concluding pages of this book. How and whether it might be possible to secure the consent, or at any rate, acquiescence, of the Northern majority to a peaceful evolution towards national unity remains an uncertain question—and reunification achieved other than peacefully would ensure lasting discord affecting the whole of Ireland, rather than anything that could properly be called national unity. All that can be said is that the prospect of reunification without violence had by the start of 1972 emerged as a possibility strong enough to warrant practical consideration and to call for serious study.

First of all, some 'non-starter' solutions should, perhaps, be ruled out. Thus the proposal sometimes canvassed in Britain, and occasionally even in Ireland, for a re-partitioning of Northern Ireland should be excluded. The politico-religious geography of Northern Ireland is much too complex to make any such solution worth considering. While there is a rather higher proportion of Catholics in the West and South of Northern Ireland, than in the North and East of the area, there are, nevertheless, about 200,000 Catholics in the North-East corner of Northern Ireland—Antrim, North Down, Belfast and North Armagh. Thus even if the boundary were re-drawn to include only those parts of Northern Ireland in which there is an overwhelming Protestant majority, less than 10% of the land area of Ireland, there would remain within this enclave 200,000 Catholic hostages—well over half of them in Belfast itself. This problem could no doubt be overcome by a transfer of populations, but the hardship this would entail would be immense and the resultant all-Protestant enclave would by the standards of modern European civilisation be a political monstrosity. This kind of solution assumes that the differences between Protestants and Catholics are of a permanently irreconcilable character; that these two communities of Ulster people are so inherently different and mutually hostile that it is hopeless to conceive of their *ever* living together in peace. Even the events of the years from 1969 to 1972 do not warrant such a deeply pessimistic conclusion.

Another proposal for a boundary change—the inclusion within Northern Ireland of the three Ulster counties now in the Republic—has been put forward by the Provisional Sinn Fein organisation as a means of persuading Unionists to accept reunification. This solution would, however, be highly unlikely to prove acceptable to the majority of people in the three Ulster counties in the Republic, and it is, of course, specifically designed to threaten the position of the Protestant community within the area of Northern Ireland. Protestants who might accept participation in a United Ireland if they retained their own provincial autonomy within the present territory of Northern Ireland, where they have a clear domestic majority, would not be attracted by a proposal which with the faster growth of the Catholic population of these areas, would threaten at a fairly early date their submergence as a minority in an overwhelmingly Catholic Ireland. Moreover, as the Provisional Sinn Fein proposal envisages four provincial parliaments within a federal Ireland, the Ulster province, within which the Protestants would have a tenuous and impermanent majority, would at the level of the federal institutions find itself in a minority of one-in-four—whereas if the existing Northern Ireland State federated with the Republic, the balance in population terms would be only two-to-one against Northern Ireland, and Northern Ireland might reasonably hope within such a twin-State system to be accorded equal representation at, say, the level of the Upper House, as is accorded in certain other federations (e.g. the United States of America) where the lower house of parliament is constituted on the one-man-one-vote principle.

Thus there seems to be nothing to be gained by playing around with the existing boundary; for good or ill, it exists, and if a federal system is to be created, it is more likely that agreement can be reached on the basis that this boundary would be let stand, than on a basis that involved a radical change in it.

The concept of a federation of the two existing Irish political entities has its difficulties, of course. There appears to be a general sentiment in the Republic in favour of such a solution, however—at any rate, no voices have been raised to protest that a united Ireland must be a unitary State, and most discussion has either explicitly or implicitly been based on the concept of an autonomous Northern Ireland region within a unified but not unitary 32-county Irish State.

This general acceptance of the concept of an autonomous Northern Ireland region depends, however, upon agreement on a reconstitution of the system of government within that region along lines that would be acceptable to the minority and would guarantee human rights, viz. on the pattern suggested in the immediately preceding chapter. This would leave the following questions to be settled:

1. The nature of the special relationship, if any, that would exist between a united Ireland and Great Britain.
2. The guarantees that the Northern Protestant community would have for their rights within a united Ireland.
3. The kind of Constitution required for a United Ireland.

4. The steps to be taken to ensure that the ending of Northern Ireland's present relationship with the United Kingdom, and its participation in a United Ireland, would not adversely affect agricultural incomes, employment in industries such as shipbuilding, social welfare benefits, or living standards generally.

5. The changes that would, in the meantime, be required within the Republic to persuade Northern Protestants that an association with the Republic within an Irish Federal State could be acceptable.

The last of these points will be considered first, in the concluding pages of this chapter, leaving the other matters over to a final chapter, for the creation of sufficient goodwill within the Northern Ireland Protestant community to enable a constructive debate to start on participation by the North in a federal Irish State will certainly require concrete evidence on the part of the Republic of a willingness to establish conditions within its own territory that Northern Protestant opinion would find broadly acceptable.

A clear distinction must be made here between more immediate changes required within the Republic to create a favourable atmosphere for future discussions, and the eventual changes in the present Constitution of the Republic that would be required to make it acceptable as the Constitution of a federal Irish State. While some matters will come up for consideration under both headings, this distinction is an important one, which emerged clearly towards the end of 1971, in the limited public debate that surrounded the decision to establish an all-party Committee in the Republic to discuss Northern Ireland policy and possible relevant constitutional changes.

The sensitivities of Northern Protestant opinion with respect to laws and practices in the Republic have been outlined earlier. At this stage the only issue is what changes are necessary to prepare the way for constructive discussions on eventual reunification. The central problem here is the influence of the Catholic Church in the Republic on social and legal issues within the political forum. This is only minimally a matter of constitutional and legal provisions: much more important to the Northern Protestant is the evidence of indirect influence wielded by the authorities of the Catholic Church, either in preventing laws being enacted, or in securing the administration of laws in a manner favourable to what its authorities regard as the interests of the Catholic religion.

The formal constitutional and legal changes called for are, indeed, relatively few. The provisions of Articles 44.1.2—'The State recognises the special position of the Holy Catholic Apostolic and Roman Church as the guardian of the Faith professed by the great majority of the citizens'—would clearly have to be repealed, but as Cardinal Conway has said that he would not shed a tear at its deletion from the Constitution, and as only one member of the Dail—a rural Labour Deputy— has criticized its proposed repeal, this creates no problem.

Secondly, it would be desirable as an indication of goodwill towards the Northern Ireland legal position on divorce, to delete also the provision of Article 41.3.2 of the Constitution— which forbids the enactment of any law granting a dissolution of marriage. The making of such a constitutional change *might* suffice to meet Northern Protestant opinions on this matter, without going beyond this to introduce actual divorce legislation in the Republic, for divorce is a matter of jurisdiction and, as is evident from the legal position with respect to divorce in England and Wales and in Scotland, different divorce laws can exist within a non-federal State, and all the more so within a federal State, as Ireland on this hypothesis might in time become.

There will be those who argue that divorce is a human right, and that failure by the Republic to make provision for this 'right' would make more difficult reunification on a federal basis, even if Northern Ireland could retain its own divorce law, and power to modify this law in future. But the concept of divorce as an absolute human right is an arguable one, if for no other reason than because the divorce laws of every State are different, allowing the dissolution of marriage for widely differing reasons, and with widely different conditions attached. A human right must surely be something more precise than a vague provision of this kind, differently interpreted from State to State. Moreover, although the question of divorce is frequently raised in connection with the question of reunification, divorce is in fact disapproved of in varying degrees by all the Protestant Churches in Ireland, and is frowned on by a high proportion, possibly a substantial majority, of their members; although, of course, this does not mean that they would wish their view to have the force of law. The introduction of divorce in Northern Ireland is of relatively recent origin; apart from the traditional system of divorce by Act of Parliament, which applied to the whole of Ireland up to and after the division of the country and the establishment of the Irish Free State, it was only in 1939 that divorce through the Courts was introduced in Northern Ireland. In these circumstances it is possible that the genuine feelings of Northern Ireland people on this matter would be met if pending reunification a change in the Republic's Constitution were effected that made it clear that reunion would not interfere with Northern Ireland's freedom of action in relation to divorce laws, although some will feel that the Republic should go further in this matter.

Abortion, an issue sometimes raised by British commentators, and rather oddly included in Mr. Wilson's late 1971 proposals for a solution to the Irish problem, is not an issue with the bulk of Northern Protestant opinion, although there is some sensitivity about differences in obstetrical practice between Catholic and Protestant or public authority hospitals. Easier abortion has not hitherto been a significant issue within Northern Ireland, and accordingly should not create a serious problem in relation to proposals for reunification.

The Republic's laws on censorship and contraception are highly contentious issues with Northern Protestant opinion. Moreover, since unlike divorce, what is involved here is the movement of goods rather than legal jurisdiction, and as, presumably, in a united federal Ireland it would be proposed to eliminate customs controls between the two parts of the country, some solution must in any event be found to divergences in practice in these matters when a negotiated settlement is sought. It seems sensible, therefore, to initiate changes in the Republic in advance of such a settlement, as part of a programme designed to show Northern Protestant opinion that the will to reunification on an acceptable basis is genuine.

The scale of minority support in the Republic for changes in the law on contraception, demonstrated by a public opinion poll in April, 1971, which posed the issue in the context of the Republic alone, without reference to the question of reunification, suggests that if the issue were re-posed as part of a 'package' designed to create a favourable climate for reunification, it would have the assent of a majority; especially if safeguards and limitations on free sale, not adverted to in the poll, were spelt out.

In the case of obscene literature the contentious issue is the method of control rather than any disagreement on the need for some form of control. Perhaps because the censorhsip system of the Republic has applied not only to obscene printed matter but also to works 'advocating' artificial methods of birth control, thus enforcing what Protestants regard as Catholic morality on this issue, it has got a bad name in Northern Ireland. It may also be that the mere fact that the system of control in the Republic is different from that in the North, and is called 'censorship', has helped to make it a bone of contention.

The removal of the control over books advocating artificial forms of birth control would go some way to meet Northern objections, but it may be worth considering whether the Republic's pre-censorship system is worth maintaining, in view of its controversial character, now that it is in practice virtually limited in application to books which, by reasonable standards —such as may be shared by many Protestants in Northern Ireland—could be regarded as pornographic and thus amenable to a normal legal process. Such a process could be implemented in accordance with regional norms, but subject to some overall supervision to prevent local outbursts of excessive illiberalism from interfering with the sale of works which by the general standards of the time in Ireland, or in the relevant part of Ireland, would not be regarded as obscene.

In other words the real issue is not now so much a divergence of view between North and South as to what kind of books should be banned—local divergences of this kind can and do exist within the legal systems of unitary States such as Great Britain—but rather the method of control. A national pre-censorship system is objectionable in principle to many Northern Protestants, for reasons that are not necessarily entirely logical, and raises issues as between North and South which a normal police-type control on a regional or local basis would not raise. As this latter type of control could well yield similar results in the Republic to those at present achieved through pre-censorship a reversion to this latter system, employed in the independent Irish State during its early years, could well provide a solution to this problem—if accompanied by provisions to eliminate the ban on books advocating certain methods of birth control. In considering such an arrangement it must be borne in mind that the attitudes of many Northern Protestants to pornography is as close to that of Irish Catholics as to that of

British public opinion, so that the problem of divergence of standards in this matter is probably less acute than the controversy over the *method* of censorship might suggest.

It is in the educational sphere, however, that the influence of the Roman Catholic Church is seen by Northern Protestants as most pervasive. At the same time the educational systems of the two parts of Ireland, despite the differences that have grown up between them in the past half-century, retain basic similarities; both have post-primary public schools operating in parallel with denominational post-primary schools; and in both areas primary education is denominational. In Northern Ireland, however, the acceptance by the Roman Catholic Hierarchy of the principle that one-third of the members of the management boards of Catholic post-primary schools in receipt of 80% capital grants should be representatives of the relevant Local Education Authority to be nominated by the Minister for Education, has created a situation very different from that in the Republic.

But although Protestant fears of Roman Catholic ecclesiastical influence in education are real and run very deep, the concern of the Church of Ireland in particular, especially in the Republic, to retain its own denominational schools at both primary and post-primary level has meant that there has been relatively little pressure for a diminution of the denominational element in education. In these circumstances, it is not easy to see what precise changes in the educational system in the Republic could be initiated, or are required, in order to offer reassurance to Protestant opinion in Northern Ireland.

The other important area where a change in the present arrangements in the Republic would be regarded as an earnest of the sincerity of its people's wish for a reunited Ireland acceptable to the Protestants of Northern Ireland is that concerning the Irish language. To Protestants in Northern Ireland the refusal to grant School Leaving Certificates to those who do not pass in Irish, the Irish language requirement for entry to the Colleges of the National University of Ireland, and the Irish language requirements in relation to recruitment into and promotion within the public service of the Republic, appear discriminatory against people of their tradition, few of whom in past generations were Irish speaking. It can, of course, be argued (in this as in every other instance where changes are proposed in the Republic as an indication of willingness to meet the point of view of the majority in Northern Ireland) that the present arrangements in the Republic are without prejudice to quite different arrangements that might apply in the examination system or public service of a federal Irish State. But this will not appear convincing to Northern Protestants, even those with goodwill towards an eventual reunification of the country, for they see their co-religionists in the Republic as being adversely affected by these language requirements, and regard the provisions under which these requirements are imposed as penal in character vis-à-vis people who do not belong to the native Gaelic tradition, and as indicating an attitude of mind opposed to the kind of pluralist society that they would expect to find in a united Ireland.

A change of policy in this matter, as in the others referred to above, seems desirable, therefore, if the Republic is to show itself to the Protestant people of Northern Ireland as liberal and open-minded, concerned to meet their reasonable requirements, and determined to treat the existing small Protestant minority in the Republic in a manner satisfactory to Protestants of the North. It is worth noting that the principal Opposition party in the Republic, Fine Gael, is in fact committed to these reforms affecting the Irish language.

Summing up the specific steps that might usefully be taken in the Republic at this stage as an earnest wish of its people to seek a reunification of the country in terms that could be acceptable to Northern Protestants, the changes that seem to be most needed are the repeal by referendum of the constitutional provisions on the special position of the Catholic Church and divorce; amendment of the law banning the import and sale of contraceptives; a modification of the system of dealing with obscene printed matter, substituting a new version of the older system of control by prosecution for the existing censorship system and the removal of Irish language requirements in examinations and in recruitment for, and promotion within the public service.

Consideration should also be given to implementing in the Republic reforms introduced in Northern Ireland since 1969. Some of these reforms may be less necessary in the Republic than in Northern Ireland, but they nevertheless could have a useful part to play, and Northern Catholics and Protestants alike would be reassured to know that the Republic was keeping in step with Northern Ireland in this respect. The matters concerned include the appointment of a Commissioner for Complaints and a Parliamentary Commissioner for Administration; the appointment also of a Police Authority; and steps to extend the impartial system of public appointments in the Republic to posts not now covered, e.g. rate collectors, sub-postmasters, etc. In these and other reforms the guiding principle should be the provision of absolute guarantees of fair and equal treatment for all citizens regardless of religion, or politics.

Finally, in all legislation dealing with matters that may be at issue between the two religious communities, the guiding principle should be the general welfare of all, rather than the moral consensus of the majority community. If that principle is followed then the problems hitherto created both North and South as a result of legislation influenced by the views of the predominant group in the area concerned, will be avoided in future.

Such a programme, if implemented generously, and if accompanied by an evident willingness on the part of the Catholic Church authorities and the political parties in the Republic to offer concrete re-assurance to Northern Protestants that a united Ireland would not, as they fear, be dominated by the Church authorities, or by the teaching and influence of the Church, would create conditions favourable to an eventual serious discussion of a programme of reunification. Some kind of declaration of intent by churchmen and politicians could make a great contribution here.

Pressures favouring a development of this kind have been the impact in the Republic of the implication by Rev. Ian Paisley in his December, 1971, radio and newspaper interviews that changes in the Republic might affect the attitude of Northern Protestants towards the North-South relationship, and the proposals by Richard Ferguson, the former Unionist MP who since his resignation has joined the Alliance Party, for a new, non-sectarian Ireland, which in the spring of 1972 began to make a significant impact in the Republic. The refusal of the Fianna Fail Party Conference early in 1972 to accept a proposal to postpone constitutional reform until negotiations started for a united Ireland reflected the growing willingness of public opinion in the Republic to seek a solution in the form of a new kind of society, rather than by an attempt to impose the Republic's cultural values and Catholic ethos on Northern Ireland. Up to May, 1972, however, this approach was still being resisted by the Fianna Fail Government which appeared, however, to be swimming increasingly against the tide of public opinion on this issue. Even if the all-party committee of the Dail announced in December, 1971, but not set up until May, 1972, was envisaged by the Government as a body that should concern itself with changes to be made as a part of an eventual negotiation, it is quite possible that its work will lead to proposals for interim changes in the Republic along the lines suggested above. Fresh pressure in favour of such changes will come from the proposal in the British initiative of March 24, 1972, to have regular plebiscites in Northern Ireland on the reunification issue.

10. The Shape of a New Ireland

IF ACTION were taken in the Republic along the lines outlined in the preceding chapter, with a view to showing the sincerity of its people's wish for a united Ireland in which Northern Protestants could participate on terms acceptable to them, and if this contributed to a shift in Protestant opinion in the North that made possible constructive discussion of progress towards an eventual political union between the two parts of Ireland, what kind of solution might emerge from such a discussion?

In the last chapter, four major issues were mentioned in this connection—the nature of any link a united Ireland might have with Britain; steps to safeguard employment and living standards in Northern Ireland; guarantees for Northern Protestants' rights; and appropriate constitutional provisions of a federal character.

A LINK WITH BRITAIN?

Various suggestions have been put forward from time to time concerning a possible link between a united Ireland and Great Britain. These have ranged from Northern Unionist dead-pan suggestions that the Republic should seek reunification by rejoining the United Kingdom, to vague talk of a special relationship. Mr. Harold Wilson in his proposals towards the end of 1971 suggested that a united Ireland should be a member of the Commonwealth, and that some kind of declaration of allegiance to the Queen should be open to Northern Unionists.

This is a sensitive area so far as the Republic is concerned, both at the level of symbols and at the level of reality. Many people in the Republic are conscious of the adverse effects that the continuing relationship of economic dependence on Great Britain has had throughout the half-century of independence and are chary of anything that would perpetuate or even strengthen this link. And the symbols of British rule, such as the Crown, have such unhappy connotations for the great majority of Irish people, that any attempt to revive them would be unacceptable to this majority.

This attitude does not, however, necessarily rule out either close social ties between the whole of Ireland and Britain, or the maintenance of certain symbols for the Unionist population of Northern Ireland for so long as they would wish to retain them. So far as social links are concerned, these exist already. Under the provisions of the Ireland Act, 1949, Irish citizens enjoy the privileges of British citizenship in the UK, including the right to vote at both general and local elections, and reciprocal rights are given to British citizens living in Ireland, subject only to the limitation of exclusion from voting at General Elections. (This limitation arises from an interpretation of the provisions of the 1937 Constitution which, however, it has recently been authoritatively suggested may be incorrect.) Thus even though formal dual citizenship does not exist, the privileges of dual citizenship are in effect largely enjoyed by Irish and British in each other's countries, with minimal limitations. Thus, for example, many Irish people join the UK defence forces and free movement of people between the two countries exists on a scale and on terms that have not even been contemplated within the EEC, the only limitations being the existence of a right to deport undesirable citizens of one country from the other, and the Northern Ireland law that restricts to Northern Ireland residents the right to secure employment there—a provision which, in theory at least, operates against citizens of the UK who are residents of Great Britain as much as it does against citizens of the Republic of Ireland. (This law is in conflict with EEC legislation and will come up for review at the end of the transitional period.)

In these circumstances there would seem to be no inherent obstacle to an arrangement of formal dual citizenship as between a united Ireland and Great Britain. It should be possible to find solutions, even solutions without precedent in international relations, for problems of this kind which arise from the complex and often irrational relationship that history has imposed on these two islands.

Of course the two countries will in any event be very closely linked economically, and possibly also, in time, politically, through their common membership of the EEC.

But given the dislike shared by Paisleyites, Provisionals, and many Northern Ireland Unionist and Opposition parliamentarians alike for the EEC, given the fact that in 1972 the Community still means relatively little even to those people in Northern Ireland who accept the idea of membership, and given the fact that relations between EEC countries are still much less close in many respects, (e.g. free movement of labour and freedom of capital movements), than those already existing between the UK and the Republic of Ireland—who are also bound together by similar parliamentary and legal systems—it does not seem likely that the participation of both parts of Ireland and Great Britain in the Community will in the early years at any rate do much to reconcile Northern Unionist opinion to a new relationship with the UK.

What of the Commonwealth? The UK by entering the EEC is severing such remaining special links as it has with the Commonwealth, e.g. trade preferences with some countries, and special provision for immigration. In these circumstances the exact significance of the Commonwealth is lost on the Irish in the Republic and there seems to be some reason to believe that it doesn't, and perhaps never did, mean much to Northern Ireland. The fact that the two parts of Ireland were both in the Commonwealth during the 1920s and 1930s, and, arguably also—although to no practical effect—up to 1949, never made any difference to relations between North and South in those decades and is not likely to make much difference in the closing decades of the century when the Commonwealth has ceased to have much practical significance.

Of course the fact that it now means so little may be an argument in favour of the Republic accepting Commonwealth membership, if there is any evidence that Northern Ireland would attach any importance to thus remaining within the Commonwealth in the event of reunification with the Republic. But unless there is such evidence, Commonwealth membership might prove to be only a further complication for Ireland in a period when its main concern will be to play a full part in the EEC, and it might, therefore, be better left on one side.

Because economic dependence on the UK in the half century after independence proved so unfavourable to the Republic, and because within the EEC the general economic and trading relationship between the two countries will in any event necessarily be determined on a Community basis, there may not be much to gain from an attempt to construct a special economic relationship between a united Ireland and Great Britain. This does not mean, however, that special arrangements will not have to be made for the safeguarding of employment and living standards in Northern Ireland after reunification, and these arrangements may well involve special financial provisions of a kind unusual between sovereign States.

PRESERVATION OF EMPLOYMENT AND LIVING STANDARDS

In an earlier chapter the differences between output and average living standards in the two parts of Ireland were described and discussed, and the nature and scale of British subsidies to the province was also adverted to. From what was said there it should be clear that if the two parts of Ireland are within the European Economic Community, the political reunification of the country would not be likely to disrupt the pattern of trading and other economic relationships between Britain and Northern Ireland. The old fears that if Northern Ireland became part of a united Ireland instead of forming part of the UK of Great Britain and Northern Ireland, it would lose access to the British market, or be dragged down by involvement with a less industrialised, highly protected, and allegedly less efficient part of the country, can be seen to be without foundation. Even should a Great Britain from which Northern Ireland had separated itself politically wish to discriminate against its former province—which is clearly highly unlikely—it would not in fact be free to do so within the EEC. Even in the allocation of public contracts, Great Britain would be under an obligation to award them on a non-discriminatory basis, Irish firms whether North or South of the present border, being entitled to tender for the non-equal terms with British firms. Only where defence matters are involved could Northern Ireland lose out in this situation; one could envisage certain defence contracts being confined to firms within Great Britain, whereas at present they might be awarded to a Northern Ireland firm. This problem is not a major one in the context of the whole issue of reunification, but it could have a significant impact on a small minority of workers in certain firms, and guarantees by the British Government on this matter would have to be sought in any negotiations involving an ultimate reunification of Ireland.

Apart from this difficulty, which under EEC conditions would be a relatively minor one, the economic problems posed for Northern Ireland by reunification arise from the extent to which the area is currently subsidised by Great Britain. The extent of these subsidies was set out in Chapter 3 and their termination would have a very severe effect indeed on living standards in Northern Ireland. About half of the agricultural subsidies—those which involve prior supports—will cease to come from the UK Exchequer after entry to the EEC, and will be financed from the Community's common agricultural fund, and most of the others may be phased out at a later stage as they are replaced by Community schemes of subsidy. But the remainder of these inter-regional transfers would be affected if Northern Ireland ceased to be part of the UK.

The transfer to the Republic of Ireland of this burden—assessed at £160–170 m. in 1971/72—would increase its tax burden by 28–30%. The resultant level of taxation would be very high indeed, even by the standards of very rich countries which can afford to set aside a higher proportion of their national output for redistributive purposes.

Moreover this level of taxation would leave the people of the Republic of Ireland poor relations in their own country—taxed almost a quarter more heavily than their Northern compatriots but with an average level of social security benefits less than half those of Northern Ireland. To raise the Republic's own social benefits and health service provisions to the Northern Ireland level—leaving on one side education and capital investment in housing, etc.—would have cost a further £145 m. in 1969/70 (probably £160 m. in 1971/72) and this, together with the financing of the subsidies to Northern Ireland, would have raised the level of taxation in the Republic by almost 60%, to a level beyond that of any other country.

It is, quite bluntly, economically impossible for the Republic to take on such a burden; the level of taxation and borrowing involved would drive out capital and destroy the ability of industry and commerce to invest in future expansion, and it would moreover be intolerable to the ordinary people whose living standards would be sharply lowered by the massive transfers they would be called upon to make to the more prosperous Northern Ireland through the tax system.

This problem is not necessarily permanently insoluble. Over time the economic gap between Ireland as a whole and Britain, and the much smaller gap between the Republic and Northern Ireland, will tend to close, because growth rates have been —and under normal peaceful conditions are likely to remain— higher in Ireland than in Britain. Thus between 1960 and 1970 the average growth rate of gross domestic product in the Republic was 3.75%, or about two-fifths greater than the UK growth rate of 2.6% a year for the same period. Over the shorter period from 1964 to 1969 figures are available for Northern Ireland also. They show that during this five-year period the average growth rates of GDP in Northern Ireland and the Republic were 4.1% and 3.9% respectively, as compared with 2.35% in the UK.

It is, of course, possible—likely, perhaps—that in the decades ahead the UK will achieve a more impressive performance than in the 1960s. But in Ireland also, assuming peaceful conditions, growth may be expected to accelerate because of the impact of EEC membership on agriculture and, through agriculture, on the rest of the Republic's economy. (In the longer run another favourable factor is the gradual change in the 'mix' of the economy, with slower-growing agriculture diminishing in relative importance vis-à-vis industry, so that even if the growth rates of each sector remained unchanged, the national growth rate, being the weighted average growth rate of all sectors, would tend to rise). A growth rate approaching 5% has been projected by the Government of the Republic for the period of transition to EEC membership, accelerating to over 5% after 1977. This assumes, of course, that Ireland, with Britain, becomes a member of the EEC.

It may well be, therefore, that in the decades ahead the Irish economy, including Northern Ireland, might grow at a rate in the region of 5% a year, while that of the UK would expand at something like 3½% a year, the ratio between the two growth rates being similar to that experienced in the 1960s, but both being at a higher level than during that decade. If that happened then the gap between the two islands in living standards would be bridged in about a quarter-of-a-century.

That this is not wild speculation can be seen by reference to what actually happened in the 1960s, when average material living standards in the Republic (measured in terms of average personal consumption per head, adjusted to allow for the somewhat higher price level in the Republic than in Britain) rose from about 50% of the UK level to about 60%, thus bridging in ten years one-fifth of the gap between living standards in the two States. Allowing for the somewhat higher level of living standards in Northern Ireland—earlier the North/South differential was estimated at something over a quarter—the average level of material living standards in the island of Ireland in 1970 was about 67% that of Great Britain. An annual growth rate of 5% in the national output of the island of Ireland, in conjunction with a 3½% growth rate in the UK, would bridge this gap in between twenty-five and thirty years.

Moreover if Northern Ireland, with its initial somewhat higher level of living standards, achieved the 5% growth rate projected for the Republic, then the gap in output and living standards between this region and Great Britain, which has necessitated large-scale subsidisation by the UK Exchequer, would be bridged in twenty years. That Northern Ireland is capable under normal conditions of achieving a faster growth than the UK is evident from its experience in the period 1964–1969, referred to above.

Under these conditions it would be possible to contemplate a gradual phasing out of the UK current and capital subsidies, which, if spread over a period of twenty to twenty-five years might be achievable without imposing any hardship in the people of Northern Ireland or requiring the less prosperous Republic to finance for the people of Northern Ireland social benefits or capital investment which it could not afford for its own residents. Admittedly the feasibility of this concept depends upon a necessarily hypothetical differential between Irish and British growth rates in the years ahead, but this is so much in accord with past experience in these two countries during the 1960s, and, indeed, with the experience of other parts of Western Europe where, with the aid of regional policies, the less-developed peripheral regions have been achieving significantly higher growth rates than the more centrally-located regions nearest to them,[1] that it seems a reasonable basis upon which to work.

There is the further consideration that the problem of different levels of social security provision in different parts of the EEC may well come up for consideration by the European Community in the years ahead. A logical corollary of common agricultural and regional policies, and of the proposed common economic and monetary policy, is a common social policy. Indeed it is difficult to see how a Community, inter-dependent in agricultural and regional matters, and with a common monetary policy evolving towards a common currency, could avoid introducing a common social policy also. It must be admitted that there has so far been little indication of a move in this direction, but the Community has had its hands full both internally and externally hitherto, and the restlessness of the trade unions about the lack of progress in social policy is bound to become a more potent force for change in the years ahead. At this point one can do no more than note the possibility that the evolution of the enlarged Community could well within the period of a couple of decades that has been mentioned above, bring it to the point where the responsibility for ensuring a common standard of social security provision would be accepted as being one to be undertaken by the Community as a whole, on the same basis as its agricultural and regional policies, and its existing very limited Social Fund, which is confined to assisting with problems of redundancy and re-settlement arising out of the transition to free trade.

From the point of view of the UK Government, a solution of the problem of Northern Ireland, involving an immediate end to the liability to keep significant armed forces in the area, could well make worthwhile the acceptance of a commitment to provide social security subsidies on a diminishing basis; a commitment that would be no more onerous at the outset, and less so as time passed, than the obligation they would carry if Northern Ireland remained an integral part of the UK during these decades. An arrangement of this kind would seem to be both a necessary and a feasible part of any solution involving a gradual transition from the present situation to

[1] See 'L'Evolution Régionale dans la Communauté—Bilan Analytique, 1971', Office des Publications Officielles des Communautés Européennes, especially Table R I.

one in which Northern Ireland and the Republic were united on a federal basis in a new Irish State.

GUARANTEES OF PROTESTANT RIGHTS

Perhaps the area of least difficulty in any attempt to find a peaceful path towards a new politically united Ireland is that of guarantees for civil and human rights. That is not to say that there are not political problems within the Republic with respect to changes in the Constitution, laws or practices of that State in certain matters. Conservative opinion amongst Roman Catholics, especially in rural areas, does not relish changes in the Republic's arrangements in respect of such matters as divorce and contraception. But reluctance to make changes within the Republic, which is itself far from being an insuperable obstacle to such changes but represents rather a cause of delay, is accompanied by a very general, one might almost say universal, acceptance of the principle of maintaining existing legal provisions and practical arrangements in Northern Ireland in respect of these sensitive matters after reunification. No voice has been raised at any stage in favour of seeking to apply within Northern Ireland the provisions in the Republic's laws to which exception is taken by Northern Protestants, and the provision of guarantees of what Protestants in Northern Ireland deem to be their civil or human rights in matters of this kind, poses no problem. This would of course involve several constitutional changes in the Republic—to eliminate the articles recognising a special position for the Catholic Church and forbidding the enactment of laws for the dissolution of marriage—but few doubt that these changes would be carried without difficulty in the context of specific proposals for reunification, if indeed they are not implemented well in advance.

It is probably true to say that most people in the Republic think almost unconsciously of reunification in federal terms. There is an often unstated assumption that, at least for an indefinite period after the problem of political unity has been resolved, Ireland would be a federal State, and that Northern Ireland would continue to have its own laws and its own administrative system, Political unity would then take the form of the transfer to an all-Ireland Parliament and Government of the powers that are at present exercised by Westminster, subject to any modifications in the distribution of powers that might be agreed to be desirable. Thus on the assumption that the internal government of Northern Ireland was reformed on a basis acceptable to the minority there, such as has been outlined in Chapter 9, most people in the Republic would not wish to interfere in any way with the internal laws and practices of Northern Ireland within a politically united Ireland, and once necessary reforms are made to secure the rights of the minority within Northern Ireland, opinion in the Republic would be happy to provide binding guarantees for the preservation of such features of the Northern Ireland system as Northern Protestants may regard as necessary—e.g. the right of divorce, the right to contraception, the right to maintain present educational arrangements, the right to be free of any obligation to learn the Irish language. As has been mentioned earlier in this chapter the right to retain dual British and Irish citizenship might also be agreed.

How might these and other similar rights be guaranteed to the Northern Protestant community? Any proposal that did not actually involve the continued presence of the British Army on Irish soil would be likely to find acceptance in the Republic. As in the case of guarantees of civil rights to the Northern minority, referred to in Chapter 9, a number of alternative methods are open: a judicial guarantee to be enforced by a specially constituted constitutional court; a guarantee through a blocking vote in the lower house of the Federal Parliament or through an arrangement involving the Federal Senate in which both parts of the country might be equally represented, or even international guarantees, involving the EEC, the Council of Europe or the United Nations. The desire of the people of the Republic to reassure the Northern Protestant majority in this matter is strong and genuine, and once minority rights in Northern Ireland are secured, the guarantee of the rights of the majority there, as they conceive them, is unlikely to pose any problem.

Constitutional Arrangements

As has already been stated, the idea of a federal solution is already well-established in the Republic and commands widespread, if ill thought out, acceptance. Few people in the Republic have given any thought, however, to the consequences that would flow from acceptance of such a system. Many people may be influenced unconsciously by the model of the present arrangement between Westminster and Stormont into thinking of a subordinate parliament in Northern Ireland combined with an enlarged version of the present Dail and Senate. The alternative of *two* subordinate legislatures and government, one for each part of the country, together with an all-Ireland Parliament and Government, has probably not impinged on many minds.

Would the Westminster/Stormont model, translated to Irish conditions, in fact provide a satisfactory solution? From the point of view of the Northern Protestants it seems highly improbable that the kind of representation they enjoy at Westminster could provide an acceptable model for an all-Ireland arrangement. It is one thing for Northern Protestants to be a small minority in a Westminster Parliament, the vast majority of whose members ultimately come from the same religious tradition, but to be a simple minority in a predominantly Roman Catholic all-Ireland Parliament would be a quite different matter. At the same time, although people in the Republic have not given much thought to the matter, there could well be dissatisfaction with an arrangement under which all the affairs of the Twenty-Six Counties would be determined by a parliament in which one-third of the representatives came from the other part of Ireland, while the people of the Twenty-Six Counties were in turn denied any similar voice in the internal affairs of Northern Ireland.

The truth is that while little or no thought has been given to this matter, a federal system between two areas such as the Twenty-Six Counties and the Six Counties, whose population ratio is only two-to-one, would have to be constructed on a more logical basis than the arrangement that exists at the moment between Westminster and Stormont. The interests of both communities demand this. What this means is, of course, that there would in future have to be both a parliament for the Twenty-Six County area and a Parliament for Northern Ireland, together with a Federal Parliament, and a similar arrangement at government level. For a small country, which will also have to provide for its representation in the institutions of the European Community, this is a rather cumbersome and top-heavy arrangement. Could it be streamlined in any way?

If the federation were constructed on the kind of model that is provided by certain other federations such as the United States, representation in the lower house of the Federal

Parliament could be proportional to population, leaving the Senate to provide a mechanism, if desired, for guaranteeing the rights of the smaller part of a United Ireland, e.g. by equal representation of the two areas in that Chamber. Bearing in mind that the total volume of legislative activity at the two levels—regional and national—would be unlikely to be much greater than would be the case in the parliament of a unitary State, and bearing in mind the short distance between Dublin and Belfast, it might be worth considering whether the problem of duplicate parliamentary representation would not best be overcome by arranging for the same ratio of representation vis-à-vis population in both parts of the country, and for constituting the two regional lower houses of parliament, meeting jointly, as the Federal Assembly. Similarly if the two upper houses had an equal *number* of seats, the two regional Senates meeting together could constitute a federal Senate.

The alternative to this arrangement—quite separate regional and federal chambers—would impose a heavy representational burden on a small country, especially when combined with the need to provide for representation in the European Parliament, which before long may also be a directly elected assembly. So long as representation in the European Parliament continues to be by indirectly elected parliamentarians, chosen by their national parliaments, the problem of triple representation which this would otherwise pose, could, perhaps, be overcome by electing to the federal and European Parliaments an appropriate number of members who would *not* be members of the regional parliaments, but who would be divided between, the two regions in the same proportion as the Federal Chamber to which they were elected.

The identity between the regional and federal parliaments might not so easily be reproduced at government level, however. The tensions between the two communities in Northern Ireland, which render necessary for a time at least a community government of the kind outlined in Chapter 9, do not exist in the Republic where there does not appear to be any valid reason for abandoning the normal type of parliamentary democracy with a majority government. A federal government could not easily be composed of a simple union of two such divergent types of regional government. In any event, while the tasks of regional and federal legislatures can be combined, that of regional and federal governments cannot so readily be

merged. A federal government different in personnel from the
regional governments, thus seems desirable, although one
should not, perhaps, rule out in principle an element of common
membership between the two.

How should this federal government be chosen? If the rights
of what would in these circumstances become the Northern
Protestant minority in the new Ireland were adequately
guaranteed against the powers of the federal government and
legislature, there would not appear to be a strong reason for
departing at the federal level from the system of majority
parliamentary government, although one could envisage the
emergence of a sense of frustration amongst the Northern
Protestant population if over a period of years none of the
representatives elected by them to the federal parliament
found their way into government. This would be likely to
happen, however, only if the representatives chosen by this
one million people held themselves aloof from the general
party system, remaining a separate 'unionist' group. This is
unlikely to happen, however—the cohesion that would lead
to such a result had already started to disappear even before
reunification has become a live issue. Moreover if this cohesion
were in fact retained, then isolation in the federal parliament
would have as its corollary a continuing dominant role in the
Northern Ireland regional parliament and government. It may
be doubted whether in the light of these considerations it
would be necessary to make any special provision for the role
of the one million Northern Protestants in the Federal Government.

A more real issue is that concerning the distribution of
functions between federal and regional authorities. It cannot
be assumed that the existing allocation of functions between
Westminster and Stormont would necessarily be satisfactory.
On the contrary, arrangements acceptable in that context are
very unlikely to prove adequate for a federal system in which
two areas of unequal size, the smaller of which is the richer, are
linked together politically.

Within a unitary all-Ireland State significant transfers of
resources would occur as between the North-East and the
rest—just as such transfers take place at present in the Republic
between the East and the rest of the country. But if such
transfers on a significant scale were required to be a feature
of the Federal Irish State from the outset, this would prove a

deterrent to acceptance of reunification by the Northern majority. It would seem, therefore, that some system of gradually phasing into a normal redistributive system would be needed.

Again, a major function of a national or federal government is the allocation of capital through public capital programmes. Within an Irish federal system some guarantees could be required by Northern Ireland that it would receive an adequate share of such allocations. This problem is further complicated by the fact that, as was mentioned earlier, Northern Ireland at present benefits from very substantial injections of capital as well as current transfers from Great Britain. As a result its house building programme is on twice the scale of that of the Republic, in relation to population, and its roads programme is even more lavish. Even assuming agreement on the maintenance of such capital flows on a gradually diminishing basis, as proposed earlier, it would be necessary to provide some kind of guarantee that the allocation of national capital resources through the federal public capital programme would be such as to ensure that Northern Ireland did not lose out under this heading after reunification. This would be all the more necessary because of the evident danger that after the first flush of enthusiasm for reunification, public opinion in the Republic might become restless at having to allocate to Northern Ireland a disproportionate share of the federal capital programme so that this region could continue, with the aid of the gradually-diminishing UK subsidies, to build more houses and more roads than the Republic!

One solution might well be a continued segregation of the two regions' capital programmes for a long transitional period i.e. making public capital investment a regional responsibility. But in view of the nature of public capital investment, financed in large measure by government borrowing, such an arrangement might not prove satisfactory, for the ability of the regional governments to borrow abroad, as would be necessary to finance part at least of the capital programme, might be very limited by comparison with that of the federal government.

It is clear from this that the financial arrangements for a federal Irish State would need very careful consideration, if the people of Northern Ireland were to be assured that participation in such a State will not work to their economic disadvantage.

Turning to particular areas of public authority responsibility, many questions arise as to possible allocations of functions between federal and regional governments. On the one hand certain areas of responsibility are potentially sensitive, e.g. education; on the other hand external affairs, external defence, the postal, telephone and telegraph services, the collection of taxes to finance federal services, and the organisation of statistical information, would appear to be clear-cut and non-controversial cases for federal control. Moreover within the EEC context monetary, agricultural, industrial transport and external trade policy would have to be organised on a federal basis because they would be so closely linked to Brussels. Other aspects, however (including possibly such matters as the administration of agricultural services within the framework of federal and EEC policy) could be undertaken at either federal or regional level. Where a choice exists there may well be a preference both North and South to retain control at regional level, in the first instance at any rate.

The allocation of functions between federal and regional governments presupposes a new structure for the public administration in Ireland—the emergence of a new federal civil service, comprising sections of the existing civil service organisations in Northern Ireland and the Republic, and certain parts of the British administration located in Northern Ireland, e.g. the Post Office services. This is bound to pose some problems, especially where, as in the case of external affairs and defence, no such sections of the public administration at present exist in Northern Ireland, and special steps would have to be taken to ensure adequate representation for Northern Ireland residents in such sections of the federal public service.

What of internal security? This problem admits of alternative solutions. It could be organised regionally, in Northern Ireland by the Community Government and in the Republic by the regional parliamentary majority government. Alternatively a mixed federal force could be established, welding together the different traditions in a body that might come to command the respect of all sections of the community. Whatever the solution the body responsible for maintaining peace and order in sensitive areas in Northern Ireland should be of mixed composition, so far as the two communities there are concerned, and under impartial control.

So little thought has been given on either side of the Irish border to the kind of issues raised above that there is very little to go on in attempting to suggest how the allocation of functions between federal and regional administrations might best be arranged, in the interest of an agreed solution. Naturally enough the Northern majority has given little consideration to this subject, which up to the beginning of 1972 only a few enlightened and farsighted public figures from that tradition had been willing to contemplate seriously. And as the test of any solution must be its acceptability to at least a large minority of that tradition, who together with the Catholic minority in Northern Ireland might come to form a majority of opinion in Northern Ireland favouring a new united Ireland, this deficiency is not easily remedied. Many details of an ultimate federal structure would have to be left open for discussion, and even the general shape of the optimal solutions to some problems is not discernible at this stage.

Enough has, however, been said to indicate both the amount of work remaining to be done and also the fact that to the kind of problems posed by the issue of Irish reunification, constitutional solutions can be found, albeit in some instances of a novel character. More important, perhaps, at this stage is to consider what transitional stages might be possible between the present situation, and a federal Ireland.

For in the Republic there is widespread recognition—signs of which are to be found even in policy statements by the IRA groups and by such figures as the former Minister, Neil Blaney —that any transition to a united Ireland must be gradual, and must take full account of the fears and preoccupations of the Northern majority.

A number of proposals have been put forward for interim solutions, which would accept the principle of Irish unity, but postpone for a period significant practical changes in political authority within the island. One suggestion, put forward by Neil Blaney, has been for a Council of Ireland, with a chairman alternating annually, to have responsibility for Ireland's external relations, while leaving domestic affairs for the time being to the governments and parliaments North and South. Another, put forward by Richie Ryan, spokesman for External Affairs of the Fine Gael Party, is for a condominium—a sharing of sovereignty by Ireland and Britain over Northern Ireland for a period. The fact that such proposals have come from politicians in the Republic is a clear indication that in the search for solutions that will meet Northern Protestant susceptibilities, virtually nothing will be ruled out.

At the same time those Northern Protestants who are now facing up to the issue of Irish reunification are clearly anxious that any solution agreed shall not be just an interim one, to be re-opened again later, with further risk of disturbance and confusion. Any interim solution such as those outlined in the preceding paragraph should therefore be designed to evolve towards a specific federal solution, with an appropriate timetable. For that reason, in so far as any discussion of a united Ireland is appropriate at this stage, in advance of evidence of a willingness of a majority of the people of Northern Ireland to contemplate such a development, the discussion of the shape of the ultimate federal solution is not premature.

Deliberately this book has avoided any discussion of the stages to be gone through before this whole subject can be discussed fruitfully. At the time of writing many obstacles stand in the way of any negotiations between the violently conflicting interests involved. This book has been written on the basis that these immediate difficulties must in time be overcome, and that a stage will be reached, sooner or later, where the problem of a new Ireland, politically united, will come under practical scrutiny. However remote it may appear to many, we must start to prepare for that moment.

Epilogue

No BOOK by an Irishman on this subject could fail to reflect to some degree his personal background; it would not require much detective work to establish from internal evidence that the author of this book is a Roman Catholic from the Republic of Ireland. Nevertheless in writing it I have tried to avoid intruding personal views of prejudices, and have endeavoured to write as objectively as possible. I feel entitled, therefore, at the end, to indulge myself a little, by expressing, briefly, without the inhibitions that have governed what I have written above, my own personal views on a few aspects of this question of Irish reunification.

I am of mixed ancestry—half Ulster Scots and half Southerner. Apart from some immediate relatives, almost all my relations in Ireland are Northern Protestants, with whom throughout my childhood and ever since I have had close ties. This personal inheritance makes it impossible for me to accept either the *simpliste* theory that there are two quite separate nations in Ireland, or the equally *simpliste* counter-theory that Ireland is one nation with a single neo-Gaelic, Roman Catholic culture, to which all citizens North and South should conform.

History has created in the island of Ireland one nation with several different cultures, and the concept of a mono-cultural nation-State simply does not fit the Irish case. Those who have pursued this illusion in the Republic have done violence to our history, and have been the real partitionists, for they have raised new barriers to reinforce the far from insuperable obstacles that existed in 1920. Politics in the Republic as in Northern Ireland took a wrong turning after 1920, and it has only been since the mid-1960s that—partly thanks to the Second Vatican Council—the tragically rigid attitudes of Irish

Catholics have begun to dissolve and to be replaced by something that in good conscience one could describe as a Christian approach to their fellow-Irishmen.

In this situation the enemy of progress towards peace and reconciliation is self-righteousness. So long as all concerned are content to harp on *their* particular grievances and to refuse even minimal understanding of their opponents' attitudes, so long will the crisis last. In this situation the job of politicians—and of journalists and writers—is above all to try to see the other man's viewpoint, and to explain each side to the other. Any man who from a position of influence collaborates with or contributes to the mutual misunderstanding of polarised groups, betrays his trust.

Between 1969 and 1972 most politicians in the Republic at least avoided making the situation worse; despite occasional back-sliding the time-honoured tradition of using Partition as a political football was effectively abandoned by the great majority of those in positions of responsibility in public life in that part of Ireland.

But although in this negative way political leaders on the Republic generally acted with responsibility, it cannot be said that up to the early months of 1972 we have given the strong positive lead towards reconciliation in a new, non-sectarian, Ireland that is so much needed. Fear of loss of support from conservative Catholic voters has inhibited too many political voices from being raised in support of the kind of New Ireland proposed by Dick Ferguson. It is to contribute towards filling this gap that I have written this book.

I believe the time has come for all Irish politicians who genuinely believe in a united Ireland, so organised that people from both communities will feel equally at home within it, to speak out and to lead the people of Ireland towards this goal. We may find that some of our people reject this lead, and that in the process existing political structures become cracked or even shattered; this is a price we shall have to pay if called upon to do so. The issues at stake cut right across the familiar boundaries of politics in the Republic; in every party there are people who look forward with enthusiasm to a non-sectarian, pluralist, united Ireland; and in every party there are others whose vision still ante-dates the Second Vatican Council, and who cherish the Catholic-orientated society that grew up in the independent part of Ireland during the 1920s and 1930s.

Within the ranks of the Catholic clergy—and the episcopacy—as within the political parties a similar division exists.

Hitherto the Republic has been dominated by two great orthodoxies—the pre-Vatican II orthodoxy in the Catholic Church, exclusivist, and triumphalist—and the neo-Gaelic cultural orthodoxy, which sought to impose on a very mixed Irish society the traditional cultural values of the rural Irish-speaking tradition. In the 1960s these two orthodoxies were challenged, and in the face of events in Northern Ireland from 1968 onwards, they came under intense pressure. The British initiative of March 24, 1972, with its provision for periodic plebiscites in Northern Ireland on the issue of Irish reunification, introduced a new element into this situation—a time-limit for reform in the Republic. Those who, before March 24, had fearfully soft-pedalled the need for radical changes in that part of Ireland, found themselves after that date open to the accusation of undermining the possibility of a relatively favourable outcome from the first such plebiscite. Whereas before the British initiative it was the liberal forces in the Republic which had always been on the defensive, open to accusations of being anti-Irish and anti-Catholic, from that moment onwards it was the conservative forces which came under pressure, their responsibility for maintaining the partition of Ireland clearly pin-pointed for the first time. For this reason I believe that in the Republic as in Northern Ireland March 24, 1972, will in time be seen as a crucial turning-point.

What kind of Ireland should Northerners and Southerners be seeking to create together in the years and decades ahead? Many English people, secure in the belief that their society is the best of all possible societies, assume that Ireland's aim should be to reproduce this in miniature. Few Irish people would agree. The strength of the religious tradition in Ireland, however distorted it may have been by bigotry and intolerance, adds a dimension to Irish society that is lacking in Britain. Again, the smaller scale of Irish society, and perhaps also something in the character of the Irish people, has made Irish society much more intensely personal in its orientation than society in Britain; as was mentioned earlier, even Irish cities are in sociological terms collections of villages rather than anonymous concrete jungles.

Freed from the narrowness and bigotry of the traditional 'orthodoxies', North and South, Irish society will therefore develop along very different lines to that of Britain. Transplanted to Irish soil the British liberal tradition, and the international socialist tradition, will blend with the specifically Irish inheritance of the island's people and with their deeply-rooted system of Christian values, to create something quite distinct.

Eight years ago, long before the first signs of a Northern crisis emerged, I tried to visualise the kind of Ireland that we should be trying to build.[1] Having first discussed the need to synthesise the Christian, liberal and socialist traditions, I went on to say:

'This society would be specifically Irish in its inspiration, proud of its origins and determined that the culture and way of life of Ireland should have a high reputation in the world. This Irish society would draw on the mixed origins of our society—Gaelic, Anglo-Irish, Ulster-Scots and English—and would be neither exclusive nor sectional. It would glory in our mixed inheritance, despising none of it, and elevating no part to a position of pre-eminence over the rest.

'In such a society narrowness and intolerance would be regarded as vices meriting social disapproval. Bigotry in any form would not be tolerated; sectarian organisations dedicated to promoting the personal temporal advancement of members of a particular religion would be universally frowned upon.

'Relations between North and South would be based on whole-hearted acceptance of the principle that political unity must be preceded by a unity of hearts. . . .

'In the social sphere the obligations of man to his fellow-man would be recognised as a fundamental fact of social life; provision for social welfare as the first duty of a community to its citizens. Property would be a trust to be guarded and justified; the accumulation and handing-on of great wealth would be seen as a social evil tending to corrupt alike those who accumulate and those who inherit.

'Art and culture would command public esteem; and the preservation of open spaces and of historic features in our towns and countryside would be given a high priority. Votes would be sought and found by striving to preserve rather than to destroy.

'Such a society would be open. . . . Educational opportunity would be a primary feature. . . .

[1] 'Towards a National Purpose', *Studies*, Winter, 1964.

'The mingling of those holding different religious views would be encouraged. . . . Censorship would be strictly confined to the protection of the young from commercial exploitation. And youth would be encouraged to face the modern world rather than be completely sheltered from its manifestations until the moment of being thrown into its maelstrom.

'The sense of nationality enjoyed by Irish people in such a society would be simply pride in their country and their roots in it, and in the society of which they form a part. It would be neither narrow nor exclusive, containing no hatred of any other country, nor passion for revenge or self-assertion. This local loyalty would be accompanied by a sense of belonging to Europe, and by a sense of inter-dependence with the rest of the world.'

Writing eight years later I would place more stress on the need to eliminate sectarianism (which in 1964 seemed to be a dying force), and on the need to create a participatory society, responding to the Irish emphasis on the individual person and to the development of socialist thought in the 1960s. But subject to such shifts in emphasis, I believe that much of what I wrote on the eve of my entry into politics remains valid as an ideal for an Irish society that would respond to the instincts and needs of Northerners and Southerners, Protestants and Catholics alike. And to-day, in contrast to 1964, there exists a growing body of opinion in both Northern Ireland and the Republic that looks in this direction. The most urgent task of politicians on both sides of the Border in the months and years ahead will be to mobilise this body of opinion for the struggle to create a New Ireland.

Appendix I

Basis of 1971/72 Estimates of Northern Ireland Subsidisation By Great Britain

The following is the basis of the figures set out on page 56 for inter-regional transfers from Great Britain to Northern Ireland in respect of current government expenditure in 1971/72:

1. Under-attribution of Corporation Tax—The £2 m. re-adjustment was mentioned in Northern Ireland Budget Statement, 1971.

2. Over-attribution of Customs and Excise—The figure of £37 m. for this item in 1971/72 is given by Professor Norman Gibson in a letter to the *Irish Times* on March 29, 1972.

3. The figure of £57 m., and the basis of its calculation are given in the Northern Ireland Budget Statement, 1971.

4. Agricultural Remoteness Grant—Given in Budget Statement, 1971, as £1.9 m.

5. Regional Employment Premium Assistance—Given as £10¾ m. in Budget Statement, 1971.

6. Agricultural Subsidies—Given as £30 m. in the Budget Statement, 1971.

7. Imperial Contribution Shortfall—The increase of £15 m. to £85 m. is a private estimate of the author's and should be regarded as an approximation rather than a firm figure.

Appendix II

Comparison Of Social Welfare Provisions In Northern Ireland and Republic of Ireland, 1969/70

No adequate study has been made of the cost of bringing social welfare provisions (including family allowances and health services) in the Republic into line with those of Northern Ireland. The matter was raised in the Dail by way of questions on November 2, 1971. The Minister for Health told Dr. John O'Connell (Question 11) that 'if eligibility for all the services here were to be extended to the entire population, the additional expenditure from public funds would probably be of the order of £30 m. a year'. The Minister said that he had no reason to believe that health services in the Republic were inferior to those in Northern Ireland, so that the only significant difference between the two parts of Ireland was in respect of eligibility.

The Minister for Social Welfare told the same deputy (Question 29) that 'our social welfare costs are now moving into the range of £103 m. which is quite a formidable sum. I would estimate that approximately half that would be required to bring our services up to the level of those in the North'. This estimate was challenged by the author, who suggested in a supplementary question that the average per capita payment in the form of social welfare payments in Northern Ireland was about 2.2 times the figure for the Republic, and that therefore the Minister's estimate of a 50% increase in cost was too low.

The author followed up this matter on subsequent occasions —November 11, Question 5; November 17, Questions 15–18; and November 25, Questions 12–27. The Minister refused to answer Questions 13–22 on November 25, however, on the grounds that the work involved in providing this information would be 'very substantial' and that he would not feel justified in asking his staff to undertake it 'even if the exercise were feasible and likely to serve a useful purpose'.

In the absence of the information sought it is possible to make only approximate estimates of the cost of applying Northern Ireland levels of benefit and eligibility to social welfare payments in the Republic. This is attempted in the following paragraphs, which relate to the financial year 1969/70, the latest period for which national accounts figures for Northern Ireland and the Republic are available at the time of writing.

TOTAL COST OF SOCIAL WELFARE

The total cost of social welfare transfers in the Republic in 1969/70 (exclusive of maintenance allowances to persons suffering from infectious diseases, rehabilitation and maintenance of disabled persons, and school meals), was £89,520,000.[1] The equivalent figure in Northern Ireland was £99,500,000.[2] As the population of the Republic in that year—2,921,000—was almost twice that of Northern Ireland—1,512,000, social welfare expenditure per head of population was 2.15 times as great in Northern Ireland as in the Republic—viz. £65.8 per head as against £30.65.

It does not, however, necessarily follow that the application in the Republic of Northern Ireland rates of benefit and standards of eligibility would cost 2.15 times the Republic's bill of £89,520,000. Different rates of unemployment and different proportions of old people and children in the population, could affect this relationship. It is, therefore, worth while comparing the benefits separately under each heading.

RETIREMENT PENSIONS

Retirement pensions in Northern Ireland are payable at age 65 for men and at age 60 for women in Northern Ireland, but retirement from regular employment is a condition of payment up to age 70. The total cost of retirement pensions in Northern Ireland in 1969/70 was £34,901,000.[3] As the total number of men over 65 and women over 60 in the Republic is almost precisely twice the Northern Ireland figure (385,000 as against

[1] *National Income and Expenditure*, 1969, Table A.19.
[2] *Digest of Statistics No.* 36, September, 1971, Table 112.
[3] *Digest of Statistics No.* 36, September, 1971, Table 114.

193,000 in 1966), it would appear that the cost of applying Northern Ireland standards of eligibility and benefit to retire- ment pensions in the Republic would be about £69,800,000. The actual cost of old-age non-contributory pensions and non- contributory old-age pensions in the Republic in 1969/70 was £29,121,000.[4] (But see next section.)

WIDOW'S BENEFITS AND GUARDIANS' ALLOWANCES

The number of widows in the Republic in 1966 was 1.87 times the number in Northern Ireland. On this basis the cost of applying Northern Ireland standards of eligibility and benefit to the Republic in 1969/70 would in this instance have been £9,550,000 as the cost in Northern Ireland was £5,133,000.[5] The actual cost of widows' and orphans' non-contributory pensions and widows' and orphans' contributory pensions in the Republic in 1969/70 was £12,400,000.[6] The fact that this figure is so much higher than the cost of applying Northern Ireland standards of eligibility and benefit to the Republic is explained by the fact that in Northern Ireland widows over the age of eligibility for retirement pensions receive pensions under this scheme rather than widows' pensions. Because of this a valid comparison can be made only in respect of the aggregate of retirement and widows' pensions. On this basis the cost of applying Northern Ireland standards of eligibility and benefit in the Republic would be £79,350,000, as compared with actual expenditure of £41,560,000 under these two headings— viz. 91% more.

UNEMPLOYMENT BENEFIT, ETC.

The average number of people in receipt of unemployment benefit or assistance in the Republic in 1969/70 was 54,750. The average number in Northern Ireland in receipt of unemploy- ment benefit or supplementary benefit in respect of unemploy- ment was 34,000. As actual expenditure in Northern Ireland on unemployment benefit was £7,521,000[5] and in receipt of supplementary benefit in respect of unemployment was £7,055,000,[7] the total amount in question was £14,576,000. As there were 1.61 times as many people in these categories in

---

[4] Dail Debates, Vol. 256, No. 12, November 17, 1971, Cols. 2267–2268.
[5] *Digest of Statistics No.* 36, September, 1971, Table 114.
[6] Dail Debates, Vol. 256, No. 12, November 17, 1971, Cols. 2267–2268.
[7] *Digest of Statistics No.* 36, September, 1971, Table 36.

the Republic as in Northern Ireland, the cost of applying
Northern Ireland standards of eligibility and benefit in the
Republic would have been about £23,465,000. As the actual
cost of Unemployment Benefit and Assistance in the Republic
was £14,824,000.[8] the increase in this instance would have
been 58%.

SICKNESS AND OCCUPATIONAL INJURIES BENEFIT

Because of different inter-relationships between these two
schemes in the Republic and Northern Ireland they must for
this purpose be taken together. There were 1.9 times as many
people at work in the Republic as in Northern Ireland in
1969/70. As actual expenditure on Sickness Benefit, Injury
Benefit, Disablement Benefit and Industrial Death Benefit in
Northern Ireland in that year was £16,969,000,[9] the application of similar conditions of eligibility and similar rates of
benefit in the Republic would have cost about £32,240,000.
The actual cost of Disability Benefit, Treatment Benefit and
Occupational Injuries Benefit in the Republic in 1969/70 was
£16,168,000,[5] so that in this instance the increase in cost is
estimated at just under 100%.

MATERNITY BENEFIT, ETC.

The number of births in the Republic in 1969/70 was 63,000
as against 32,000 in Northern Ireland—viz. 1.97 times. As the
cost of maternity benefit in Northern Ireland was £1,326,000[6]
the cost of applying similar benefits in the Republic would have
been £2,630,000. Actual expenditure in the Republic on
maternity grants and allowances was £430,000.[5]

FAMILY ALLOWANCES

The schemes in the two parts of Ireland are somewhat
different. In 1969/70 the annual rates of benefits payable were:

	Northern Ireland	Republic of Ireland April–July	Aug.–March
First Child	Nil	£6	£6
Second Child	£47	£9	£18
Third and subsequent Children	£52	£16	£24

[8] Dail Debates, Vol. 256, No. 12, November 17, 1971, Cols. 2267–2268.
[9] *Digest of Statistics No. 36*, September, 1971, Table 114.

Thus for families with one child there was no equivalent in Northern Ireland to the Republic's benefit of £6 a year. For two-children families the payment in 1969/70 was £47 in Northern Ireland and £21 in the Republic. Three-children families received £99 in Northern Ireland and £42 in the Republic. Families with four children secured £151 in Northern Ireland and £63 in the Republic. Families with five children secured £203 in Northern Ireland and £84 in the Republic.

With regard to the numbers of families of different sizes in the Republic, this can be estimated from data with respect to payments made to families of different size given in reply to another parliamentary question.[10]

The figures are set out in the table below. It should be noted that the parliamentary question did not seek a breakdown of payments as between different sizes of family in excess of four children of eligible age, and the figures for these sizes of family have had to be estimated by reference to other data on family size, using the total sum paid in respect of all families of this size as a control figure.

COST OF PAYING NORTHERN IRELAND FAMILY
ALLOWANCES IN REPUBLIC OF IRELAND 1969/70

Size of Family (Eligible Children)	No. of Families	Actual Payment in Republic of Ireland		Payment at Northern Ireland Rates	
		Per Family	Total	Per Family	Total
		£	£	£	£
One	88,500	6.0	531,000	—	—
Two	91,000	21.1	1,921,000	47	4,275,000
Three	70,250	42.2	2,967,000	99	6,955,000
Four	50,250	63.5	3,194,000	151	7,590,000
Five	(33,000)	84.7	2,795,000	203	6,700,000
Six	(21,500)	105.8	2,275,000	255	5,480,000
Seven	(10,000)	126.9	1,269,000	307	3,070,000
Eight	(5,000)	147.0	735,000	359	1,795,000
Nine	(1,000)	168.1	168,000	411	410,000
Ten	(200)	189.2	38,000	463	115,000
			£15,893,000		£36,390,000

Thus the cost of paying Northern Ireland Family Allowances in the Republic would have been 130% more than the cost of Children's Allowances in 1969/70, even after allowing for the

[10] Dail Debates, Vol. 257, No. 3, November 25, 1971, Cols. 491.

saving involved in not paying such Allowances in respect of the first child.

HOME ASSISTANCE/SUPPLEMENTARY ALLOWANCES

In the Republic in 1969/70 £1,260,000 was paid in Home Assistance.[11] In Northern Ireland 'Grants to Persons in Need' cost £13,842,000.[12] As living standards and incomes are generally lower in the Republic it seems probable that payment of such grants on similar conditions of eligibility as in Northern Ireland would have cost about £30,000,000 in the Republic in that year.

SCHOOL MEALS, ETC.

In reply to a Dail question[13] the Minister for Social Welfare stated that school meals and milk in the Republic cost £259,000 in 1960/70 and that of these provisions had been in the same scale as in Northern Ireland they would have cost £6,000,000.

CONCLUSION

The conclusions of this analysis are set out in the table below.

SUMMARY OF ESTIMATED COST OF APPLYING NORTHERN IRELAND ELIGIBILITY PROVISIONS AND BENEFIT RATES IN THE REPUBLIC OF IRELAND 1969/70

	Actual Cost	Cost on Northern Ireland Basis	Increase Amount	Percentage
	£	£	£	%
Health Services	52,420,000	82,420,000	30,000,000	+ 57
Retirement & Widows' Pensions	41,560,000	79,350,000	37,790,000	+ 91
Unemployment Benefit	14,824,000	23,465,000	8,641,000	+ 58
Sickness & Occupational Injuries Benefit	16,168,000	32,240,000	16,072,000	+ 99
Maternity Benefit	430,000	2,630,000	2,200,000	+ 512
Family Allowances	15,893,000	36,390,000	20,496,000	+ 130
Home Assistance/Supplementary Allowance	1,260,000	c. 30,000,000	28,740,000	+2281
School Meals	259,000	6,000,000	5,741,000	+2217
	£142,814,000	£292,495,000	£149,681,000	+ 105

[11] Dail Debates, Vol. 256, No. 12, November 17, 1971, Cols. 2267–2268.
[12] *Digest of Statistics No.* 36, September, 1971, Table 36.
[13] Dail Debates, Vol. 256, No. 12, November 17, 1971, Col. 2276.

So far as can be judged, therefore, the application of Northern Ireland eligibility provisions and benefit rates in the Republic in 1969/70 would in fact have involved a doubling of expenditure, amounting to about £150,000,000.

Index